THE
HOLY MAN
OF TOURS

"Rejoice, My Daughter, because the hour approaches when the most beautiful work under the sun will be born."
—Our Lord
To Sister Mary of St. Peter

(Our Lord refers here to the work of reparation to the Holy Face, which He revealed is destined to be the means of defeating atheistic Communism and restoring peace to the world).

LEO DUPONT

Born in Martinique, January 24, 1797, and died at Tours, France, March 18, 1876

This portrait was made shortly after his death and is based on the recollections of his contemporaries.

THE
HOLY MAN
OF TOURS

THE LIFE OF LEO DUPONT
1797-1876
APOSTLE OF THE HOLY FACE DEVOTION

By

DOROTHY SCALLAN
Edited by
FR. EMERIC B. SCALLAN, S.T.B.

*"And I will hide my face no more
from them, for I have poured out
my spirit upon all the house of
Israel, saith the Lord God."*
—Ezechiel 39:29

TAN BOOKS AND PUBLISHERS, INC.
Rockford, Illinois 61105

Nihil Obstat: JOHN M. A. FEARNS, S.T.D.
                    Censor Librorum

Imprimatur: ✠ FRANCIS CARDINAL SPELLMAN
                    Archbishop of New York
                    December 13, 1951

This book was originally published in hardbound in 1952 by The William-Frederick Press, New York, New York under the title of *God Demands Reparation: The Life of Leo Dupont*, with the author given as Rev. Emeric B. Scallan. (Dorothy Scallan is the sister of Fr. Emeric Scallan.)

Library of Congress Catalog Card No.: 90-70236

ISBN: 0-89555-390-2

Printed and bound in the United States of America.

TAN BOOKS AND PUBLISHERS, INC.
P. O. Box 424
Rockford, Illinois 61105

1990

THIS VOLUME IS
DEDICATED
TO THE ILLUSTRIOUS MEMORY
OF THE LATE

BISHOP CORNELIUS VAN DE VEN

without whose continuous help, encouragement and solicitude this book would never have seen the light of day. For it was the Bishop's pioneering zeal in the field of the Catholic press that urged him to establish a Diocesan Organ; and, appointing me as editor, launched me on a career of Catholic publishing.

WE HEREBY declare that we absolutely and entirely conform to the decree of Urban VIII with respect to the terms of eulogy or veneration applied to the servants of God, Sister Marie Pierre, and Leo Dupont, as well as to the Divine revelations mentioned in the present book; and, moreover, that we by no means anticipate the decisions of the Holy See.

THE
HOLY MAN
OF TOURS

"My heart hath said to thee: My face hath sought thee: thy face, O Lord, will I still seek."

—Psalm 26:8

THOU SHALT HIDE THEM IN THE SECRET OF
THY FACE FROM THE DISTURBANCE OF MEN.

— PSALMS : 30, v. 21

1

IT WAS early spring in Martinique in the year 1805, and
through the open windows of a small schoolhouse came the
chirping of many birds. A gentle breeze blew sweet scents
from peach groves and orange trees, and it was little wonder
that the class of small boys, as they tediously wrote on their
slates, grew restless hoping that the school-bell would ring
out an end to their captivity. Martinique in the springtime
was lovely, and the children were longing for the outdoors;
but the bell did not ring, and the afternoon dragged on, and
with it irksome study.

Suddenly the schoolmaster, Mr. Rochelle, rose and walked
to the door. "I shall leave you to yourselves for a while. Continue your lessons until I return," he said as he closed the
door behind him.

He was not gone very long, when the youngsters put down
their slates and began to play—loudly talking, laughing,
whistling and enjoying themselves with wild enthusiasm.
Their hilarity reached the ears of the schoolmaster at the
other end of the building. Mr. Rochelle at once retraced his
steps, but the boys, recognizing his hurried pace, were too
quick for him and they became silent, so that when the
flushed Mr. Rochelle opened the door, no one moved.

"Now, boys, I heard the disorder of this class at the other
end of the building. I see you are all suddenly perfectly
quiet, but you have not deceived me. I demand to know who
were the boys who misbehaved while I was away. The guilty
ones will rise and come to the front."

As Mr. Rochelle looked from right to left, he noticed that
in the second row, at the fourth desk, one boy promptly rose

and, looking straight ahead, marched up to the front. The schoolmaster waited a few moments and then made a second appeal urging the guilty ones to come forward. But no one joined the solitary penitent who, standing alone, peered uncomfortably at the teacher, expecting the worst.

"So, Leo Dupont, you admit that you have been a bad boy. I would expect better things from you, for it seems to me you are big enough to know better. Just how old are you?"

"I am eight years old, master," the boy admitted cheerlessly.

"Eight years old! Really, Leo, your mother will be very grieved to learn of the conduct of her son. Are you not ashamed to admit that you are the only mischievous boy in the whole class? Look at all your schoolmates here, sitting quietly at their desks. They have evidently conducted themselves so well during my absence that now they have nothing to confess. But you, Leo, have been the one black sheep among all these nice, little white lambs . . . ."

The guilty boys began to shuffle restlessly at their desks, their roving eyes betraying the guilt asserting itself in their hearts. But still they clung to their benches, refusing to admit their misbehavior. The large clock on the wall ticked away loud minutes like a clanging doom, warning the youngsters to confess before it was too late. Then the school bell rang. Relief registered on all faces, but it became evident that Mr. Rochelle was not quite ready to dismiss the class.

Pausing for a moment, he looked inquiringly into the faces of the youngsters at their desks and then announced calmly, "Ordinarily, when the bell rings, classes are dismissed—that is, provided there has been no misbehavior. But today it is a different story," he announced, biting his lips.

The room became tense with silence. All eyes were fixed on the threatening schoolmaster, who turned to Leo and said, "My little friend, since you have been so naughty today, I do not believe you deserve to remain in the company of all these good boys. So go for your hat, take your books, and be on your way home. The rest of the children will stay here."

Confused and puzzled, Leo nevertheless did as he was told. When the door closed behind him, the angry schoolmaster turned flashing eyes at the class, and severely scolded the boys for their dishonesty. "Boys, it is human to make a mistake. It is pardonable to grow restless and noisy once in a while. But to be false, to refuse to admit your guilt, that is something else—that is something I intend to punish. Little Leo Dupont is much younger than many of you boys, and yet he was the only real man among you. He rose and admitted getting into mischief. From a boy like that I expect great things."

Leo left the schoolhouse, unaware of the praise heaped upon him. He walked out into the sunshine, toward the large gate where he was met by the mulatto servant, Henri, who called daily to drive him home from school in a carriage. "But, Mastah Leo, why is yo all alone by yerself today? Where is all 'em classmates of yours?" inquired Henri, as he took Leo's books and slate, and helped the youngster into the shiny carriage.

Leo, still confused, did not know what to say, but finally managed a reply. "The schoolmaster had the rest of the boys stay at school," he said in a monotone.

"They must 'ed be bad boys. And you must 'ed be th' only good 'un today," said the faithful servant approvingly. "Yer mother will be mighty proud of yo, Mastah Leo. She'll be mighty proud to find out her boy was th' onliest one what was good today, while all th' others wus bad."

Hearing this, Leo was more puzzled than ever. He tried to explain that he was not good, that he had admitted being mischievous — but to no avail. Henri was beyond these mental gymnastics. He only spurred on the horses to get Leo home in extra-good time, for he felt he had good news for Madame Marie Louise Dupont, the widowed mother of little Leo. When the carriage drew up before the massive door of the imposing Dupont mansion, which towered majestically over one of the richest sugar plantations on the island of Martinique, Henri at once went in search of Madame Dupont.

"Mastah Leo is been a powerful good boy, Madame! All 'is classmates done hafta stay after school but him!"

Madame Dupont kissed her son and took him to the large refectory for some afternoon refreshments. "What is this good news I hear about you, Leo?" she asked.

Leo explained as well as he could what had taken place. Madame Dupont saw through the schoolmaster's method and although she said nothing of it to Leo, she was happy to find honesty blooming in the heart of this cherished son.

Madame Dupont was an exemplary Christian as well as a lady of high birth. She came from a noble and wealthy Martinique family, the Gaigneron de Marolles, and had been happily married to the illustrious Nicholas Dupont, who, weary of revolutionary excesses in his beloved France, had come to Martinique to make his home. Though of short duration, their marriage had been blessed with two sons, Leo, now aged eight, and Theobald, aged four. Widowed at an early age, with wealth and position, Madame Dupont turned all her efforts to the rearing of her two sons. To them she held up Christian virtues as the highest ideals; not only did she teach by word, but by example as well. Thus Leo, even at the tender age of eight, began to show those traits of honesty and candor that were to thrive and blossom into high principles as he advanced to young manhood.

Several years later, when the regular course of studies at the village school in Martinique was completed, Madame Dupont decided to send her son to school in the United States.

"Leo," she confided to him one day, "the reason I want you to go to school in the free land of the United States is that you shall learn there the importance of dignified political liberty and freedom of religious worship. I cannot send you to school in Paris because the times are too unsettled and Paris is too much a center of religious persecution. But as soon as conditions appear somewhat normal, I want you, of course, to study in Paris, and then to return to live here in Martinique, where you will in time inherit the family fortune. I shall miss you keenly while you are gone."

"But, Mother, I shall be back shortly," said Leo in that

heartening way of his, a manner which endeared him not only to his mother but to all who knew him.

Leo spent two profitable years studying in the United States, after which he went to France, where he was joined by his mother and his younger brother. It was a joyous reunion, made still happier by the news which Madame Dupont had for Leo.

"Son, your uncle, Count Marolles, has invited us to spend our summer vacation at his castle in Chissay."

"Great! When do we leave?"

"Tomorrow morning — that is, if you think you can be ready by then," replied his mother, teasingly.

At the castle in Chissay there was an endless round of enjoyable family life that summer. Count Marolles, like his sister, Marie Louise Dupont, was distinguished for his Christian refinement. His entire estate breathed warm hospitality, and Madame Dupont and her two sons entered into all that took place there: Mass on Sundays and holy days, the sacraments, and family devotions, as well as riding, driving, dancing, swimming, and other sports. And no one entered into the activities at the castle with as much gusto as Leo, now fourteen years old.

Then one day, a sudden apprehension fell over the castle. There was an accident on the grounds of the vast estate. Leo and his cousin Alfred were whiling away an early summer afternoon, while the count, Madame Dupont, and the others were taking their siesta.

"Let's climb up on the gates," suggested Alfred. "It's a lot of fun swinging on them," he added. No sooner had he spoken than he perched himself on the top of one of the huge iron gates that opened on the driveway leading to the castle. Atop the seven-foot gate, Alfred began to swing. Below, Leo stood and watched, leaning against a post. After a while he, too, decided to join in the fun; he climbed onto the other gate and began swinging. For a time all went on well, until Alfred was struck with another idea. "Leo, I'm going to swing right through to the other side this time. So take away your hand," he said as he pushed forward.

Leo looked at his cousin dubiously and refused to move his hand from the edge of the gate.

"Why don't you take away your hand, Leo? Next time I swing, I'll push harder, and if you don't move your hand, your fingers will get caught," shouted Alfred.

"Why should you swing so hard that you should deliberately get my hand caught by the gate?" asked Leo.

"Well, I will, I tell you, Leo. I certainly will! So hurry and take your hand away."

Something inside Leo seemed to contract. He looked at his cousin and said, "I don't think you have the nerve to swing the gate over my hand. You just couldn't do such a thing to me!"

"What makes you say that, Leo? I warn you for the last time to take your hand away or you'll be sorry!"

"I won't take it away!"

"All right, then. Here I come!"

A moment later the heavy gate swung violently forward and closed on Leo's thumb.

Alfred ran to tell his father about the accident. A physician was summoned. So badly was Leo's thumb crushed that Madame Dupont wept as she complained to her brother, "What shall become of my son, who is so obstinate and self-willed that he opens himself to deliberate suffering, and even maiming? What, indeed, shall become of him?" she cried.

Her brother, taking her tear-stained face in his hands, said, "I do not fear for Leo, my sister. It is for Alfred that I am concerned. Leo, you must remember, may have shown self-will, but only where he would be made to suffer from his act of self-will. With my son, Alfred, however, it is another matter. How could he deliberately ride over the thumb of his cousin? Have I ever given him such an example of cruelty? Leo could not imagine that Alfred would deliberately do him harm. Leo, my dear sister, believed in the humaneness of Alfred. Be happy, Marie Louise, that you have a son who somehow believes his neighbor to be better than his neighbor really is. Children will be children, but from this incident I see Leo emerging a man, a resolute man, who will one day forge a strong and determined will to achieve something great. One thing is sure. Leo will never, like my son Alfred, use his will stubbornly to swing iron gates onto living flesh, to inflict pain and suffering on another. It is my son who needs prayers. Leo will be all right."

2

AT THE age of nineteen Leo Dupont was a very attractive young man. His mother, who had in the meantime contracted a second marriage with Mr. Arnaud, a well-to-do landowner, was eager to see her son complete his education in Paris. Since the family wealth, to which Leo would fall heir, consisted of vast sugar plantations in Martinique, it was deemed advisable for Leo to pursue a course of studies that would launch him upon a lawyer's career, so that after his return he could fill some honorable post in the government of the French colony.

On the eve of his departure for Paris, Madame Arnaud had a confidential talk with him. "Leo, you are going away with Theobald to study in Paris. I am giving you your first annual allowance," she said, handing him checks and currency which at present value would be equal to $10,000.

Leo kissed his mother's hand, and then both her cheeks, as he had been trained to do from childhood. "May God reward you, Mother," he said and then deposited the money in a leather wallet.

Madame Arnaud motioned to him to be seated at her side, for she had something more to say. "Leo, this sum of money, which shall be your annual income while you and Theobald are at Paris, should be sufficient to purchase the comforts to which you have been accustomed at home. You are no longer a boy like your brother Theobald. You are now a young man in your twentieth year and it is to you I now address myself with grave parental authority. You understand that whatever you need you can have from me, for you have inherited great wealth from your father — a fortune that will soon come entirely into your possession. Morever, my personal wealth is also considerable, and it, too, will some day be yours. So, you are an independent young man who needs to court no one's favor for the purpose of gain. Use this independence for noble ends. If an impoverished or underprivileged person sometimes stoops to lie, to cheat, to misrepresent, to overreach, or otherwise to conduct himself dishonorably, he may excuse himself by saying that he was penniless and only wanted to advance himself; although it is always great folly to risk eternal happiness for perishable earthly gain. You will have no such problems."

Madame Arnaud paused for a moment, as if to survey the elegant surroundings, as if to be sure that she was making a correct estimate. She cast her eyes around the large room, looked up at the portrait of her deceased husband that hung in a massive gold frame over the marble fireplace, and then continued with striking self-assurance, "No, my son, you need not court the favor of the wealthy to advance yourself materially. You can stand shoulder to shoulder with any of them. You are heir to half a million dollars, Leo, and that is a grave responsibility as it is also a high privilege. You can use your fortune well, or you can abuse it. Your father bequeathed to you vast wealth, but remember, God gave you life and an immortal soul and He will exact from you a strict account on the final day. See to it, therefore, that you can face God with a clear conscience every night before you go to bed. Paris is reputed to be a wicked city, but it is also a city of good schools where, if you study well, you can cultivate your talents. But above all, my son, in Paris as anywhere in civilized Europe, there are churches where priests are ever ready to hear your sacramental confession and to give you absolution; and it is to sacramental confession that I wish to point with gravest concern. You and God, Leo, and the priest in the confessional are the three most important factors in life for you. Be faithful in going to confession, and all will go well with you. Remember, a spotless conscience is the greatest happiness . . . ."

"I will remember, Mother. This I promise," said Leo, and Madame Arnaud knew somehow that Leo would be faithful. She kissed her son ardently, for she loved him tenderly and knew they had to part. He was a man now and must begin to take his place in the world. But she would always love him, it could not be otherwise. Strangers loved Leo and how much more did she love him, who was his mother and who had delighted in his extraordinary personality from childhood.

Arrangements were made for Leo and his brother to occupy furnished apartments at the Hotel d'Angleterre in Paris; a choice well calculated to favor the spiritual as well as the material welfare of the Dupont sons, since the owner of this well-kept hotel was Madame Contour, a highly esteemed woman with whom the Duponts were well acquainted.

"Have you had a pleasant journey?" said a voice that greeted Leo as he entered the high-ceilinged lobby of the hotel. Leo at once recognized the speaker.

"Ah, Madame Contour, it is a pleasure to see you again," he said, and his words carried the amount of familiarity and measure of calculated correctness that made his neighbor understand that in all dealings with him there would be a refined geniality but also a measured reserve. Leo Dupont was simply not the type of young fellow one would approvingly slap on the back, or one to whom others would run, yelling, "Hi, well, look who's here! How've you been, old pal?"

Madame Contour, a lady of rare accomplishments, was in her true realm as she greeted Leo. She remarked to herself that the boy had grown into a very handsome man, one to whom the world would beckon with open arms to enjoy its pleasures, for she saw a young aristocrat who was tall, had dark hair, and warm brown eyes shaded by long silken eyelashes.

"But, Mr. Leo," she began, "I did not quite expect to see you grown into a young man so soon. It seems not so long since I last saw you."

"It is four years, Madame, since we were in Paris for a visit," replied Leo. "I was only about sixteen then."

"And now you are twenty and taking your place in the

world as a man. Is that right?" she asked, with a becoming smile. Leo, altogether unembarrassed, replied, "Yes, Madame, that is correct. Of course, I have been somewhat on my own since I was sent to school in the United States, and then again when I attended college at Pontlevoy, here in France. But then I was at boarding school and that made a difference, you understand."

"Indeed, I do understand. Now you are altogether on your own, a young man living in Paris, the capital of the world. You are, so to say, for the first time in your life the master of your own house and of your own soul, completely."

Madame Contour noticed a flicker of gravity cross Leo's face when she said 'and of your own soul, completely.' But Leo had no intention of entering upon any serious topic of conversation, especially on this occasion, and so he forced his temporary gravity to give way to another smile.

Just then, Theobald stepped into the lobby.

"Theobald, come here to meet Madame Contour," said Leo.

"Welcome to your new home, Mr. Theobald." said the hostess invitingly as she looked at the younger Dupont. "I hope you are not too tired from your long journey."

"I am afraid my younger brother *is* somewhat tired, Madame," answered Leo.

"In that case I must not detain you any longer. If you will follow me, I shall show you to the rooms especially prepared for your arrival," she said, as she motioned the servant to carry their luggage. "Take those two valises to Mr. Dupont's apartments on the second floor."

As the party ascended the wide, carpeted staircase, Madame Contour could not refrain from drawing comparisons. These two boys, Leo and Theobald, how different they were one from another! They came from the same family, they both enjoyed the same prestige, the same wealth, the same environment, and the same high training. Yet one stood out above the other as a church steeple towers over the humble huts of a village. Theobald was just another boy, but Leo was a personality, who, at twenty, was so arresting in his deportment, in the way he flashed his eyes, in the way he carried himself, in the way he took the lead in any situation, there was no doubting that his place in the world would be important. If wealth, high birth, and excellent schooling were in themselves sufficient to produce an outstanding personality, mused Madame Contour, then both Leo and Theobald would have stood shoulder to shoulder with each other. But there was such an apparent difference between the two that one would think they came from different worlds. Madame Contour could not restrain her reverie — "Leo Dupont, if he came from the lowliest hut, would become a giant among men of endeavor. May God keep him in this large city of Paris, so full of vice and pitfalls," she sighed as she left the travelers to unpack and rest after their long ocean voyage from Martinique.

A week later, Leo registered for a course of public lectures at the University, and also enrolled for a course of reading under a private tutor. He wanted to be a man of letters as well as of the legal profession, and so he would study the classics so he could take a place among the elite of his day.

His courses of study settled, Leo now proceeded to attend to the matter of his wardrobe. He decided to consult with some reliable haberdashers to make certain that his clothes would be correct.

"I am a student at the public lectures. Please show me the proper clothes to wear for my classes," he said to the proprietor of an elegant shop in the Rue Colombier.

"Yes, sir, right this way. I presume you desire the latest in Parisian styles?"

"Yes, I do. Please show them to me," said Leo, who knew he could afford the best. There was no need for him to live on a budget, or to hunt for a bargain. He was a citizen of Paris now, and he hoped to make an impression on its brilliant society.

"These light gray woolens with the stripes are very fashionable this season, sir," offered the haberdasher, pointing to a suit displayed behind a heavy glass door. "But perhaps they seem a little, well, shall I say, too modern?" continued the proprietor, who thought he detected an intent seriousness in the youthful face of his customer which bespoke a more conservative taste in clothes.

"Are these striped woolens the latest?" Leo asked pointedly.

"Oh, the very latest, sir!"

"Then that is precisely what I want. And now, please show me some evening clothes also. I am invited to a ball at the winter place of a count . . . ."

"Yes, sir, this way, please!"

And so Leo, dressed in the most fashionable and elegant clothes, could be seen in the lobby of the Hotel d'Angleterre; and Madame Contour, noticing his flawless attire and polished manners, really began to worry about how he would fight against the temptations of Paris.

During the brilliant social season that followed, Leo Dupont was received into the first circles of the aristocratic society of the day. He was invited to a succession of balls, where he danced in such graceful fashion that the finest of French young womanhood, noticing him, concealed their admiration with difficulty.

That Leo was not in the least averse to the attentions lavished upon him by the cream of French society can readily be seen from the fact that he returned again and again to these great houses for continued entertainment. Many outstanding families began to make overtures, seeking him as a son-in-law; but there was always an insurmountable barrier. Leo Dupont, young, wealthy, and brilliant, had a definite urge to become acquainted with the world. He wanted to know what people did and said, and though he enjoyed dancing, and singing and dining in refined society, he was not ready to make a permanent arrangement. To marry one of these socialites meant to be launched on an endless pursuit of gaiety and pleasure — and that was not what Leo wanted just now. To marry meant to settle down for life and Leo knew he was not ready for so serious and irrevocable a step. It was one thing to dance with the best-dressed and the most beautiful girl at the ball, but it was another thing to take a partner for life. The business of marriage was an earnest one and Leo did not close his eyes to this reality. But he had an education to complete, and he wanted a position in life first.

If Leo was the center of attraction at balls and soirees, he was no less proficient at daytime sports. Healthy and vivacious, he found swimming and the chase splendid outlets for working off some of his excess energy. Not only did he swim with an excellent stroke but he could perform aquatic stunts skillfully and when the hunting season arrived, he was among the fastest and most enthusiastic riders.

One day he came to the hotel lobby in search of the doorman. "John, do you know what I need very much and do not as yet possess?"

"I cannot imagine what it could be, Mr. Leo, for it seems to me you have about everything."

"You are wrong, John. I don't have everything," he objected playfully.

"Well, if you say so, sir, I must be wrong. But it seems to me that when you procured for yourself that exquisite cabriolet and, horse, the like of which there are no finer in Paris, driven by a young student of twenty-one, well, Mr. Dupont, I said to myself, now that young aristocrat has everything . . . ." John rubbed his hands, for Leo was the prize patron, the most elegant resident of the Hotel d'Angleterre, and as an observant doorman, John took great pride in waiting on this handsome man of the world.

"You have eyes, John, but you see not. You notice my new cabriolet and my horses, and, if I may say so, they are fine enough equipage. But did you ever stop to realize that I have no groom, when every man of my station has a jockey or two?"

"But, Mr. Leo," said John. "You have a servant, that boy Luke who waits on you. Must you have a groom besides?"

"Of course I must have a groom! I should have an indoor servant and an outdoor servant," he answered, looking at his patent leather shoes and wondering if the polish on them was high enough.

"Yes, Mr. Leo," dejectedly acquiesced the doorman who, accustomed to frequent tips from Leo for the smallest services, saw himself partially displaced by a groom who would ever be at his master's side. For a moment he intended to plead his cause, to assure Leo that he would always be there to serve him at the door, but he relinquished this idea for he could see Leo was in dead earnest about a jockey. He thought he knew someone who could fill the position and he now felt it his duty to inform Leo about him as a gesture of appreciation for all the tips he had received. "Mr. Leo, I know a boy, a street-sweeper, whose name is Clement. I think he would make you a fine groom. Of course, he'd have to be cleaned and spruced up for the part, but I believe you'd be fond of him. He's about twelve years old."

"John, fetch him to me as quickly as you can," said Leo at once.

Clement proved to be a prize jockey. He was a strikingly good-looking boy when washed and accoutred for his new job. Leo was highly pleased with himself. Now he had a groom. He was a gentleman of the world, a Parisian in the fullest sense. His cabriolet could be seen from a distance, gleaming in the sun, and his horses were equally well groomed, the brass fittings glittering like pure gold. It paid a man to have a hired servant like that jockey, Clement. Somehow everything was turning out for Leo Dupont just as he had wished. Could any man want more? He was twenty-one, a resident of Paris, a guest with a standing invitation at the great houses and palaces, a sought-after student of the Parisian schools — and now he had a groom all for himself! There was nothing more to be desired, he told himelf.

But just before he fell asleep that night he had a vague presentiment. What was that theory about cycles? When a pinnacle is reached is there not to be expected a period of possible reversal? But Leo was unwilling to give place in his heart to anything that suggested unpleasantness. He had no grounds for nurturing presentiments, he told himself, appeasing his doubts. Everything was wonderful! Life was thrilling! He even had a jockey! And what was more, he went to sleep with a clear conscience, just as his mother had counseled him. Only last Saturday he had been to confession and to communion. He didn't have a thing in the world to worry about.

3

Not even the oppressive heat Leo knew would descend on Paris in midsummer could induce him to make any plans that would take him away from the French capital to some cooler and quieter retreat in the country. Having spent two years in Paris, the gaiety-loving Leo was convinced there existed no greater pleasure and no higher social life than that in its midst. Here he had his many friends and his entertainments and here in Paris and its suburbs he would stay. When the heat and humidity grew too excessive, he could have Clement drive him in the new surrey through the cool Bois de Boulogne, where he was sure to meet his university companions with whom he would spend entertaining hours.

School having just closed, Leo decided to drive to the woods for a day's outing, and so he instructed Clement to be at his door early the following morning. For some reason, Clement failed to arrive. Leo consulted his watch three times and then, disappointed and rather agitated, he donned his hat and went down to the lobby.

"John, have you seen Clement this morning?" he asked the doorman.

"No, Mr. Leo, there hasn't been any sign of him here today. I've been here since seven this morning and would surely have seen him if he came in."

"I don't know what to make of it. He has always been most punctual. This is the first time he's late."

"Well, sometimes there's an unavoidable delay, Mr. Leo. Maybe Clement just isn't to blame."

"Be that as it may, this thing is spoiling my outing. It's a glorious spring day and I meant to be in the Bois de

Boulogne by now. Why must these things happen just when I had my heart set on a day outdoors? It's annoying, I tell you!"

It was nearly high noon when Leo finally heard Clement's gentle knock on his door.

"Come in, Clement," he said briskly.

"Good morning, Mr. Leo," said Clement sheepishly, as he entered and silently closed the door behind him.

"Did you say 'good morning'? It seems to me you should be saying 'good evening' instead. Clement, why have you not come on time?"

"Well, Mr. Leo, it was like this. You see, I had to go to the meetin'."

"What meeting?" demanded Leo.

"Mr. Bordier's, sir. He called us this morning and told us all to come for the instructions. I didn't have time to come here first to get your permission, so I jist sort of went...."

"What on earth are you talking about, Clement?" demanded the vexed master, whereupon the frightened little jockey proceeded to explain that Mr. Bordier was a fine gentleman who instructed a group of street cleaners and chimney sweeps in Christian doctrine, to prepare them for the sacraments. "And if we know all our answers jist right we'll make the holy communion in September," he finally concluded.

Leo Dupont was not gullible. He was a man of the world, and an ex-chimney sweep was not likely to have Leo's full confidence without an investigation.

"Are you telling me the truth, Clement?"

"Yes, I am, Mr. Leo. If you likes, I can fetch you to Mr. Bordier. He's a fine gentleman and you'll see for yourself I'm tellin' the truth!"

"Well, I shall be delighted to meet your fine Mr. Bordier, Clement. It ought to prove quite an experience. When is your next instruction?"

"Friday, sir. We must learn lots mighty fast if we're goin' to be allowed to receive the sacraments. That's what Mr. Bordier told us."

Leo Dupont's interest was sufficiently stirred and he decided to go to see for himself about the Christian doctrine classes. Who in the world would interest himself in gathering chimney sweeps and street urchins from the slums of Paris, in stifling hot weather, to teach them Christian doctrine?

Promptly on the appointed Friday, Leo went to the address Clement had given him. To his great surprise, he found a group of poorly clad boys sitting on benches, answering catechism questions put to them by a well-dressed gentleman of about thirty-five. This evidently was the astonishing Mr. Bordier. Leo listened to the class and he studied the teacher attentively. When the boys were finally dismissed, Leo went up to the instructor.

"Sir, my name is Leo Dupont. My jockey, Clement, who sits there in the third seat, informed me on Wednesday that a certain Mr. Bordier teaches Christian doctrine to street urchins and I came to be edified."

Leo's deportment was characterized by those refined manners which were fast winning him the title, "Marquis of Politeness," an honor to which he was not in the least averse.

Mr. Bordier smiled and then introduced himself. Yes, it was all true. Mr. Bordier belonged to the Congregation of Mary, a society that took an earnest interest in combating the evils of the terrible French Revolution.

"And you mean to tell me that laymen carry on the priestly work of imparting Christian doctrine?" asked Leo.

"Indeed they do!"

"But I was more or less inclined to believe that preparing youngsters for the sacraments was the exclusive realm of priests and nuns . . . ."

"To administer the sacraments *is* the realm of the priesthood. No layman can replace the anointed in this field. But surely you know what the revolution did to religion in France, and of what momentous importance it is to carry on the lay apostolate?"

"I am not altogether uninformed, sir, but perhaps I do lack a good deal of perspective on the subject. You see, I come from the colonies, from Martinique; my parents moved there when the worst ravages of the revolution began to shake France."

"Then what you know is merely hearsay. If you had been here in France to see the horrors of the Commune, if you or your parents had seen what the irreligious mobs perpetrated here, you would not be asking me why laymen are taking a practical role in imparting religious instruction."

"You are so well informed, Mr. Bordier, that I should like to know you better. Perhaps I am detaining you from some engagement now, but if you will do me the honor of a visit, I shall be anxious to arrange one at any time convenient to you. I live at the Hotel d'Angleterre."

"I'll be delighted to come, say the Sunday after next?"

"Splendid! Not this coming Sunday, then, but the one following. Is that right?"

"That's correct," replied Mr. Bordier.

Taking courteous leave of his new acquaintance, Leo walked away and found Clement waiting for him at the street corner.

"Clement, you can have the rest of the day off. Go study your catechism as Mr. Bordier told you. I shan't be needing you any more until tomorrow."

"Thank you, Mr. Leo. Thank you very much!"

Leo walked back to his hotel in deep thought. He decided to take his lunch alone and then go in search of a former school friend who had recently been ordained a priest and who was stationed in Paris. Leo had never forgotten the extraordinary personality of this brilliant scholar who finished first in his class, and who now, as Father Frayssinous, was making a name for himself by his inspiring oratory. Since the unusual Mr. Bordier had roused Leo's slumbering mind to ponder higher things, he decided that Father Frayssinous was just the right person to approach.

"It is not just for a friendly visit or to speak of our college days that I came here today, Father," Leo at once confessed after the two retired to a small rectory parlor. Looking straight into the calm, intelligent face of Father Frayssinous, Leo lost no time coming directly to the point. "Something happened today, Father, to show me I am lagging behind while others, looking ahead, are going forward . . . ." Leo paused for a moment and then added, "I allude to the important matter of salvation. While I merely drift along, others, taking advantage of various opportunities, are acquiring great merit for heaven . . . ."

Father Frayssinous wondered when he heard the fashionably attired and elegantly mannered Leo Dupont grapple so seriously with his conscience; showing no trace of that shallow embarrassment that almost universally characterized the young and old, the poor and rich of his time whenever the question of the state of one's soul was discussed. With complete frankness, Leo went on telling Father Frayssinous about his pursuits of learning, of fine dress, of elegant friends, and especially of his latest worldly satisfaction, the handsome uniformed jockey, Clement.

"And now that I had secured a jockey, I was well pleased with myself, Father, thinking I had at last every desire of my heart — when suddenly I was brought face to face with a contradiction. Clement, the last and most cherished of my worldly ambitions, turns into a symbol of reproach. How strange." Leo shook his head and smiled wryly.

"What do you mean, Leo? What has this Clement done?" asked the priest, perplexed at the sudden turn in the conversation.

"Oh, he has done nothing, Father, nothing whatever. It is only that Clement, whom I secured to satisfy my worldly ambition, Clement, who, as the groom at my side, completed for me that desirable setting, that final pinnacle in fashion and elegance which I fancied went into the making of a Parisian gentleman—yes, this Clement, through a force of circumstance, suddenly hurled me into a world I never expected to learn about, especially here in gay Paris. You see, Clement brought me face to face with my own soul . . . . But don't look so amazed, Father. I know I sound like one who has suffered a bad dream, and it may seem like one to you, but to me it is dread reality. Let me explain . . . ."

Leo related the incident that led to his acquaintance with the astonishing Mr. Bordier. "Just think of it, Father, I meet a gentleman of fine circumstances, Mr. Bordier, who gathers dirty and neglected chimney sweeps from the gutter to teach them catechism and to prepare them for the sacraments! And suddenly I see myself as I am. Oh, I managed to have Clement sought out because I wanted an outdoor servant to add to all my other worldly possessions, whereas Mr. Bordier, on the other hand, seeks out Clement, not to hire him, mind you, but rather to hire himself out to Clement without charge, to serve Clement's spiritual needs. Now, there's the rub, as the poet Shakespeare would put it. Mr. Bordier is farsighted. He is working for heaven. I am near-sighted. I work only to satisfy my earthly ambitions. And yet, we both have only one lifetime in which to work for eternity. When that one lifetime is finished, we'll be given no second chance . . . ."

"Leo, you have been granted an excellent grace to understand this. One such heavenly light is sufficient to launch you on the road to true sanctity. That is the way many of our greatest saints began their spiritual ascent!" Father Frayssinous talked to Leo for a long time. He felt his words would not be lost nor his counsel left unheeded.

Finally, when the bell rang for vespers, Leo apologized for his long intrusion. "I must not take your whole afternoon, Father. But, believe me, you have done me a world of good." Leo rose to take his leave.

"You have not taken my time, Leo. You have shared it. I am very happy at everything you told me. Do come again," he said, as he escorted the handsome aristocrat to the door.

But Leo seemed to have something more on his mind and on the threshold he paused as if to speak.

"Yes, Leo, do you want to ask me something, perhaps?"

"Yes, Father," answered Leo, as he looked down to the floor, studying the pattern on the small faded rug in the corridor. "I just wondered, do you think I ought to dismiss Clement, maybe? I mean, I could do without a jockey."

"No, Leo, I do not advise that. By employing Clement you give him a respectable position and you keep him off the streets."

"But isn't it a sort of vanity, I mean, my having Clement?"

objected Leo, determined to press for a logical conclusion, no matter what it might cost him.

"Not in your case, Leo. You see, you are not merely pretending to be a gentleman of position, you *are* one. Again, you are not hiring Clement to appear as one who is wealthy, you *are* wealthy. Situated as you are, you can afford to have a servant or two. Besides, since Clement was the instrument through whom you became acquainted with Mr. Bordier, who in turn made you reflect so deeply on your soul, would it not be a sad recompense to discharge Clement now and leave him jobless?"

Leo smiled his broad, cheerful smile. "Very well, Father, I'll keep Clement, and just between the two of us, believe me, I'm very glad you're allowing me to keep him with a clear conscience . . . ."

Father Frayssinous smiled back broadly, but inwardly he began to wonder how soon or through what circumstances God would begin to ask Leo to sacrifice his prized possessions, one after another. At present, however, he felt it his duty to assure Leo that there was no need to change his mode of living by giving up his jockey.

"Remember, Leo, all things work unto good to those who love God. Having servants or not having them, affluence or poverty, Leo, all things work unto good to those who love God!"

On the way back to his hotel, Leo tried to fathom the meaning of the priest's words. What did they mean? "All things work unto good for those who love God." Leo wrestled with his brain, trying to give image to the words, but without avail. Perhaps the words were too deep for him at twenty-one, too profound for his particular, as yet undeveloped spiritual estate. He would not pretend to himself to comprehend their intrinsic meaning. Well, it sufficed for him to do as Father instructed him to do. He would keep Clement. All things worked unto good for those who loved God. Yes, even having a jockey!

4

FROM ALL indications it seemed the summer vacation was destined to be an enjoyable one for Leo and he was more than eager to fill every social engagement that presented itself. Leo spent the Thursday preceeding his engagement with Mr. Bordier with a group of school friends. They drove out to Montmorency, a fashionable resort of aristocratic Parisians. Hiring small donkeys, they rode through the woods, up steep paths which afforded thrilling scenery, and along small streams of turbulent water.

Then came Sunday, the day set for Leo's appointment with Mr. Bordier. Dressed in his holiday best, Leo personally attended to every detail of the afternoon's entertainment. He even asked Madame Contour to serve his guest and himself tea in the small, but elegantly paneled parlor off the north end of the hotel lobby.

When Mr. Bordier arrived, Leo was suddenly conscious of being in the presence of someone destined to exercise a deep influence on him. Over the teacups Leo lost no time in telling Mr. Bordier of the favorable impression he was making. "Do you know, Mr. Bordier, after meeting you on Friday, I went directly to Father Frayssinous to tell him of how making your acquaintance has affected me . . . ."

"I happen to know Father Frayssinous rather well," replied Mr. Bordier in an effort to distract attention from himself.

But Leo was not to be brushed off so easily, for he understood that somehow this new friendship with Mr. Bordier was not to be merely a casual one. To be sure, during Leo's two-year stay in Paris he had spent numberless afternoons and evenings in social visits discussing countless topics and conversing about every imaginable enterprise except the one that now engaged his interest. This unusual undertaking seemed to be reserved for the special talents of Mr. Bordier, and on this particular afternoon Leo intended speaking about chimney sweeps and about whatever it was that disposed a man to undertake such activity. How did Mr. Bordier ever conceive the idea? Refined people who lived in gracious houses, the only kind Leo had met until now, somehow never made such amazing connections. Leo further observed that Mr. Bordier did not seem to be an eccentric sort of person. He looked as much the gentleman as Leo did himself, perhaps more so because the added years gave his brow a particular distinction that was lacking in the very youthful forehead of the law student. What, then, was the thing that had launched Mr. Bordier on his apostolate of teaching chimney sweeps the lessons of Christian doctrine?

"I have just never met anyone like you, Mr. Bordier," said Leo frankly.

"You are very young, Mr. Dupont. There are quite a few in our organization who do work like that in which I am interested, and who do more of it, and do it better . . . ."

"Well, if there are such men, I never had the opportunity to come into contact with them," objected Leo, smiling.

"How could you? At the Paris universities you attend it is very unlikely you would meet with any persons except those steeped in gross materialism, who obstinately refuse to see beyond the limits of mere sense perception. A large number of our French educators are either avowedly atheistic or, if they have retained the kernel of truth in their hearts and believe in God, they seem to be ashamed to admit it before their daring and brazenly irreligious confreres . . . ."

Leo looked up astonished. "You have stated the matter so correctly, sir, that I would think you had a real glimpse into what actually goes on right in our university."

"What goes on is apparent to all who have eyes to see. The unfortunate condition which has been thrown upon us with the French Revolution is steadily increasing in intensity. If there is no open bloodshed now in 1818 as there was in 1791 and the immediate years that followed, it does not mean the menace of the Commune has been overcome. Anarchy has merely taken on another aspect, that of underground maneuvering, scheming in the dark and propagandizing for gross materialism under the guise of science. That is why at our universities there is a worse threat to Christian civilization than anywhere else. There, under pretense of intellectualism, youths in their most susceptible and impressionable years are opened to the scoffing of religion; they see Christianity ridiculed by men who hold the authoritative position of professors. These wily men of forty, fifty, and sixty — experienced in the tricky terminology and slogans of their atheistic materialism — have no difficulty scoring a dark victory against the inexperienced twenty-year-old student, untrained in argument and refutation."

Leo looked up seriously at his guest and, since they were now finished with their tea, offered a suggestion. "Might we continue this interesting conversation while we go driving? My carriage is ready, if it is acceptable to you."

"It will be a pleasure," said Mr. Bordier, agreeably.

When Leo had driven out of the busy section of Paris, he pressed his guest to continue with the discussion of conditions in France. "For a layman you are remarkably well informed as to the effects the baneful Revolution had on Catholicism in France . . . ."

"In our day it is necessary for laymen to take a very vital interest in the work of the Church. This is a lesson which the Revolution has especially taught us," answered Mr. Bordier with self-assurance.

"What do you mean? Are you of the opinion that laymen can do the work of the Church better and more satisfactorily than priests and religious?"

"Not at all! Priests and religious can do the work best. But it so happens that no one understood this fact better than the revolutionists of 1791, who recognized the power of the clergy and therefore set out with sinister determination to crush the priesthood and religious. In the years of the French revolutionary terror, priests were the first to be attacked. They were hounded down, imprisoned, and guillotined daily. The result? Many among the clergy and religious left the country and others went into hiding. Priests as a class disappeared from France."

"How awful!" said Leo, dejectedly.

"Yes, and in those five or six worst years of the terror, it was left to the enlightened lay people to carry on the work of the Church, especially to give instruction in Christian doctrine and to keep the spark of faith alive. It was safer for the laymen to get around than it was for the clergy to disguise themselves and come out of hiding, although that too was often done. Young, resolute men often carried the Blessed Sacrament into prisons and brought spiritual consolation to refugees who lived in concealment. We have seen one such revolution here in France in which the layman was expected to come forth to replace as much as possible a clergy that was bound in shackles. We must be prepared for every eventuality in the future."

"I can see why you advocate a lay apostolate in France," offered Leo. "Really, the French Revolution must have been truly terrible!"

"It was the worst terror in all of civilized history. To explain it adequately would take volumes. I was a young boy when it was first launched. When the King and Queen were guillotined in 1791, I was eight years old and I shall never forget the horrors that followed. They were indescribable . . . ." Mr. Bordier stopped for a moment, but Leo pressed him to continue.

"Mr. Bordier, could you fix responsibility for the Revolution on any one particular cause?"

Mr. Bordier's face grew solemn. "My dear friend, historic upheavals like the French Revolution are not brought about by partial misconducts or by the misdeeds of a few refractory individuals. Believe me, a handful of irresponsible nobles do not cause a world conflagration. When so colossal a thing as the French Revolution actually occurs it is because overwhelming causes have reached a climax. Nothing would more satisfactorily illustrate what I intend to convey than for me to quote you a certain passage from the Old Testament. When God was about to destroy Sodom because of the wickedness there, Abraham pleaded with God, saying: 'Far be it from thee, O God, to destroy the good with the wicked. If there be fifty just in the city, wilt thou not spare that place for the sake of the fifty just?' We know the answer God gave to Abraham. God promised to spare the city if fifty just men were found therein, whereupon, Abraham, encouraged by the answer he had received, pleaded further: 'What if there be five less than fifty just? Wilt thou save Sodom for the sake of forty-five just?' To this God agreed, saying He would save Sodom for the sake of forty-five just. Abraham again prayed, even more boldly, asking God to save Sodom if forty just were found, and then if only thirty were found, finally if for the sake of twenty, God would show mercy. To this God replied that even if ten just could be found in the whole city of Sodom, for the sake of those ten just, God would spare the place. What was the result? Not even ten just could be found and God was constrained by His justice to destroy the wicked city of Sodom."

For a few moments there was a tense silence and then the speaker went on. "So it is at the time of terroristic upheavals. The balance between good and evil becomes so dispropor-tionate that inevitable chaos ensues. We see a similar excess of human wickedness at the time of the Crucifixion of Christ, though strictly speaking, the life of Christ cannot be held up as a parallel to mere human events. Yet deicide would never have become historic reality if human wickedness had not assumed gigantic and overwhelming proportions. Was it merely the fault of Pilate that Christ was unjustly crucified? Or was it singularly the envy of the chief priests that contrived to nail God to a cross? No, it was also the fault of the common people who cried out for His death: 'Crucify Him! Crucify Him!' Christ was unjustly condemned by all three dominant social factions of His day, the people, the state, and certain human elements in the church. How-ever much particular groups of society wish to escape re-sponsibility for epochal disasters, there is no evading the fact that such catastrophes are not sudden misfortunes brought about by a handful of miscreants! They are always the effect of wholesale wickedness . . . ."

Even Clement, who sat perched on the high seat of the shiny carriage, felt the reins in his hands tighten. Mr. Bordier taught the chimney sweeps very fine lessons in catechism, he reflected, but what he was now saying to Mr. Leo seemed to hold the threat of doom in its sway.

Mr. Bordier went on. "Leo, a good Catholic is not one who closes his eyes to truth in an attempt to minimize the faults of particular groups of men. When the terrible Revolution swept over Catholic France, it laid bare to the world the wounds of Catholic French society. Louis XVI and Marie Antoinette were not the only offenders caught in the social upheaval. There were also the abuses of the nobility and some of the higher clergy which numbered in all of France some two hundred thousand persons, the so-called 'privileged class.' We know that these privileged ones were almost entirely exempt from taxes and from the burdens of labor. They hired others to do all the work, mental and menial, while they themselves lived on large estates amid splendor and pomp, working not at all but squeezing out their luxuries from some twenty-five million Frenchmen who largely lived in dire poverty, forced to work for inadequate pay. As a result of these excesses, there were squalor and sickness and premature death everywhere, all while the privileged class continued to enjoy themselves.

"It is a story of shame that Christian society should ever have become so unconscientious. Among the underprivileged there were some forty thousand humble priests who worked together with the poor in the slums of the cities and in the huts of impoverished villages. No stipend was theirs, no benefice, no endowment! They were of the common people and almost without exception were left in dire need. Finally, when the revolutionary element won, there followed a period that was chaotic. The state, with a generous public gesture, made restitution to the poorer clergy who now received their legitimate stipends and benefices, those which really belonged to them and which had for so long been denied to them. But alas, as could be expected, here was encountered a contradiction. Does the world ever give anything to a clergyman, no matter how justly, without in due time exacting from that clergyman unjust tribute in return? The lower clergy, once granted their benefices by the state, were expected to reciprocate by giving unbounded allegiance to that state!

"This reached a degree of positively incredible exploitation when the state ruled that all priests were unconditionally bound to give their 'civil oath of allegiance.' When the Pope condemned these new laws of the rabid French revolutionists, excess knew no bounds. More than half the clergy refused to take the civil oath. For this nonconformity they were labeled traitors, hunted down, and when caught were sent to prison or to the guillotine.

"Those were the days when priests had to flee from France or else go into hiding. Here and there they managed to say a mass in some cellar and secretly administer the sacraments to a few who had the courage to assemble under cover. Of course, if they were discovered attending mass they were promptly marched off to the guillotine, together with the celebrant."

"Guillotined for attending mass in some quiet place?"

"Yes, my friend, guillotined for simply attending holy mass!" replied Mr. Bordier. "But there were other abuses, too. A friend of mine, a boy of sixteen, was drafted into the service of the terroristic government and was appointed a state executioner. What was he to do? His family, as well as he, were all faithful Catholics. It was a matter of either owning up to his faith and refusing to perform the bloody office of the executioner, thus betraying his family, all of whom would be murdered, or else taking his station at the guillotine every Wednesday and Sunday to slaughter innocent victims — priests, nuns, and faithful Catholics. Joseph was his name. He decided at the last moment to go to his murderous station. When he ascended the platform of the guillotine to perform his first execution, he suddenly went stark mad. He never let drop the bloody knife. He is still alive today, as mad as ever, raving violently, pronounced incurably insane in a state institution . . . ."

"How terrible!" exclaimed Leo, and then fell into silence. For a while they drove on, as if in deep reverie. Finally Leo had something to ask, "Mr. Bordier, tell me more about the Society of Mary to which you belong. You mentioned that it was composed of laymen who devote part of their time to charitable works?"

"Yes, that's correct. In addition to instructing poor children and preparing them for the sacraments, some members visit the sick in hospitals and go to prisons to bring comfort to inmates, others work to provide clothes for the destitute."

"Do you think I could join this Congregation of Mary?"

"Indeed you could. Whenever you are ready I will make an appointment for us to pay a visit to the Father Director."

The conversation was suddenly interrupted by the appearance of three youths on horseback who stopped at Leo's carriage to exchange a few words. "We recognized your jockey, Clement, and so we followed you," one rider called out to Leo.

"Looks as if you chaps were having a jolly time . . . ." Leo called back.

Then a third rider, catching up with the carriage, asked, "How did you come out after the terrible drenching at Montmorency last Thursday?" Then, not waiting for an answer, the three rode off in high spirits and were soon out of sight.

"Friends of mine," said Leo, somewhat apologetically, as he turned to Mr. Bordier. "And, speaking of the drenching last Thursday, did you happen to get caught outdoors, too?" Leo asked.

"No," said Mr. Bordier hesitatingly. "In fact, I didn't know until now that there had been a sudden downpour."

"You didn't know? Why everyone talked about the unusual storm that came from nowhere, drenched everybody, and was over in a few minutes. But maybe you were out of town?"

"No, I was here in Paris. You see, I was in church attending vespers at the time."

"In church for vespers? But it wasn't Sunday. It was Thursday," objected Leo quite positively, forgetting himself for the moment.

"I know it was Thursday. But it was Ascension Thursday!" replied Mr. Bordier.

Leo's face flushed and his spirits fell. "Ascension Thursday," he repeated to himself in a whisper. "A holy day of obligation!"

"It is growing late, Mr. Dupont, and I believe it is time for me to think of getting back to town," suggested Mr. Bordier, wondering what he had said to make his host, who had been so cheerful all afternoon, become suddenly so pensive and confused.

"Why, yes, yes," Leo forced himself to say, trying to regain his poise. "Clement, turn here, turn back to the city . . . ." he said.

When Leo was alone in his apartment an hour later, he walked to a huge mirror that hung on the wall and said aloud, "For the first time in my life I missed mass on a holy day of obligation. What is Paris doing to me that I should have grown so negligent as to completely forget the feast of the Ascension?"

For quite a while Leo fought with his conscience. Although he knew that due deliberation and full consent of the will were necessary to constitute a mortal sin, he still could not hold himself altogether excused. He began recalling what Mr. Bordier told him about the price many Catholics paid during the revolution simply because they attended mass. These Catholics had faced the danger of death each time they convened in some cellar to hear a priest say mass. Often they were caught and taken to prison or sent to the guillotine. Yet he, Leo Dupont, with full liberty to perform his religious obligations, goes to Montmorency for an excursion, completely forgetting that the day was the feast of the Ascension! Leo's conscience smote him. He must go to see Father Frayssinous. What a contradiction! Only ten days ago he had sought out Father Frayssinous to pour out to him his high aspirations. In fact, he was on the verge of giving up his jockey, so full of enthusiasm was he to enter on a life of self-denial. And today he must race toward the confessional to admit missing mass on a holy day of obligation!

Leo fell to his knees. He made a sincere act of contrition. As he knelt, he reached for the linen handkerchief in his pocket to dry two tears that ran down his cheeks.

5

WHEN SEPTEMBER arrived once more, Leo enrolled for advanced courses in the school of law. It was with studied purpose that he began to watch the attitude of his professors toward religion. He was now in his twenty-second year, he told himself, no longer a mere freshman. Moreover, having enrolled as a member of the Society of Mary, he now had the advantage of Mr. Bordier's good example, from which he was determined to reap much fruit. For Leo was not a tepid or indifferent individual who looked at good example and remained unmoved or who obstinately continued to drift along in the same old habits. He had acquired new ideals and he began to break certain unfavorable friendships and increase his fidelity to such friends as Father Frayssinous and Mr. Bordier, both of whom he strove diligently to imitate.

At the end of the first semester, Leo, having watched with alarm the ever-increasing amount of anti-Catholic propaganda being spread at the university, decided it was time to put into practical use the lessons of zeal for truth he had learned from Mr. Bordier. There simply had to be some way to take the initiative against the open attacks on religion and religious customs which made it the butt of slurring remarks at almost every lecture.

After turning the matter over in his mind for a while, Leo invited three of his classmates whom he trusted to meet in order to outline a plan.

"But what can we do?" asked one of them. "If we make any objections in class, the professors will mark down our papers and we will be retarded."

"Yes, and especially that Professor Albert whose anti-religious jibes prove only too well his deep-rooted resentments. It's simply no use . . . ."

"But it is of some use," disagreed Leo. "We must try, we must make some sort of attempt, and if we find in due time that the professors mark down our papers in reprisal for our objections to their atheism, then will be time enough to begin to count our steps. Moreover, all four of us are in good circumstances. We can afford to be put back and stay on an extra year in school, if need be." Leo paused for a moment, and his face lighted up. "My mother once told me I never needed to measure my actions to suit the temper of those in power, because I did not need their condescending patronage. I could afford to stand alone, if need be, to defend a principle. I believe this is the occasion for me to put into practice the counsel she gave me. None of you are paupers either. I want to know if you are willing to join me . . . ."

The three students hesitated a bit and then one of them spoke up. "Well, Leo, it depends on what you propose to do."

"I have it all planned out," answered Leo, and the twinkle in his eye suggested something amusing. All three pulled up their chairs closer.

"Leo Dupont, what are you up to?"

"Listen to me attentively. The little scheme I have should give us more fun than work. Here's what we'll do . . . ."

The three listened to Leo, their eyes beginning to sparkle and their expressions betraying that they were only too eager to join him in his stunt.

When classes were resumed on Monday, no one guessed that the casual remarks which the foursome made during recess periods were part of a well-outlined plan. Yet, whenever they had a chance, all four managed to drop remarks about the suppers attended by students and faculty members on Friday evenings when school was out for the week-end and parties were generally arranged.

"I think the Maison de la Riche is the best place to go for Friday night parties. That's where the outstanding professors go, and those students and alumni who really are somebody."

"Do you really think so?"

"Why, of course. Places like Raynard's and Maurice's are out of date. But Maison de la Riche, where everyone dresses in dinner jackets, is the right place to frequent. Leo Dupont, myself, and two other fellows are going to the Maison de la Riche this Friday . . . ."

That line of informative gossip went the rounds of the junior and senior classes so that the majority of the university began to make arrangements to go to the Maison de la Riche on Friday night instead of elsewhere. Even the faculty members of the lower strata began to figure on an extra expenditure to be able to dine at the Maison de la Riche. They had to keep up their prestige. If students were able to dine at Maison de la Riche, so were they. Even Professor Albert, known for his penny-pinching economies, decided that he could not afford to be absent. When Leo learned through the college grapevine that the antireligionist, Albert, could be counted on to be present at the Maison de la Riche, he began to anticipate Friday evening with even more zest.

When the appointed evening arrived, there was more than an ordinary stir in Leo Dupont's apartments. One by one, the three students arrived, immaculately attired in evening dress. Madame Contour, who happened to be in the lobby and saw the display of formality, could not suppress her curiosity. She knocked at Leo's door. "Mr. Leo, it seems you are celebrating some extraordinary occasion this evening. Can I be of any help?"

"Yes, indeed you can. We're dining at the Maison de la Riche this evening, and you can be kind enough to let us know if we pass inspection . . . ." Leo knew how to be amusing.

"Maison de la Riche? Has the student body taken to that fashionable resort lately?" she asked.

"They are beginning to be introduced to its fashionable environs, Madame, owing to Leo's premeditated little stunt," explained one of the students."

"Stunt?" asked Madame Contour, smiling.

"Yes, stunt, Madame, but we cannot tell you more. It's a secret."

Madame Contour smiled pleasantly. Young men are young once and they must have their share of sport, she concluded, as she escorted the foursome to the surrey where Clement waited to drive them on their Friday evening excursion.

"Good evening, Mr. Dupont," said the headwaiter, to whom Leo was no stranger. "You have reserved a table for four?"

"Yes, for four, in the center of the dining room," replied Leo.

"Very well! Everything is as you ordered it," catered the headwaiter politely.

The four gentlemen sauntered leisurely to their festively decorated table in the middle of the large dining room. Heads began to nod here and there as faculty members and students recognized Leo and his three confreres. Everyone seemed to be in high spirits and all were ordering fine meals. Leo and his party had purposely arrived late. Taking his time, Leo ordered a glass of sherry for himself and for his friends. He noticed students and professors as they carved their juicy beefsteaks and other meat courses. A surprise came when the foursome suddenly noticed that at the next table in full view sat Professor Albert, who from his point of vantage could not help seeing and hearing everything that was done and said at Leo's table.

Leo and his friends ordered. "Fruit compote for all of us, and then some puree of peas," said Leo. The maitre d'hotel approached to make some suggestions.

"Gentlemen," he began, "we have a fine beef roast, *au jus,* veree delicious!" He raised his eyebrows, puckered his thin lips, and then, gesticulating with his hands, he went on, "In addition, we also have veree, veree fine roast duckling with giblet dressing." Again he paused, as he prepared to offer the prize dish of the evening, "But veree most special for tonight, gentlemen, we have a roast of fresh, young, milk-fed pork which . . . ."

"Leave the pigs in their pens, Monsieur. This is Friday,

and being Christians, we don't eat meat today!" Leo's voice rang out. It was meant to be heard by his college friends, among whom were several weak Catholics; but especially was it meant for the benefit of Professor Albert, who, Leo knew, was once a Catholic also but who now sat feasting on a steak an inch thick. "So for us it will be fish, if you please."

"Fish?" stammered the maitre d'hotel. "Yes, sir, and what kind will it be?" he asked, lowering his voice as if to apologize to the other guests. It was up to him to preserve the standards of the Maison de la Riche.

Speaking in clear, audible tones, Leo named the kind of fish he wanted and then sat back in the upholstered straight chair. "George, what kind of fish shall you have?" he asked casually.

"I think I'll take flounder, broiled flounder, if you please," answered George, who also made it his business to be heard. Students and professors at adjoining tables paused to listen to what the other two would order. They had not long to wait for in distinct voices both young men ordered fish, and fish again.

The headwaiter's hand was trembling as he wrote down the orders. He wondered how many guests were watching his embarrassment.

When the fish was ready, the headwaiter decided to send an assistant to serve these Friday courses to the law-abiding Catholic dinner guests. The assistant, completely unaware of the situation — he had only recently been employed — served the fish course to Leo first and said quite casually, "I see you are of the old school. You keep the Friday abstinence . . . ."

"Yes, we observe the Friday abstinence, not because we are of the old school but because we belong to the Church which never changed the laws regulating Friday abstinence," replied Leo.

Professor Albert, who could not help hearing every word, paused and then shot Dupont and his colleagues a menacing look. They were registered in his class and he had ways of reprisal.

The rest of the meal went smoothly. If the group had rehearsed the whole scene with every actor including the concierge, the maitre d'hotel, the assistant waiter, and the guests, the effect could not have been more perfect. Leo's aim was to rebuke the false human respect of the Catholics of his day, students he knew at school who came from Catholic homes and held the true faith, but who, intimidated by irreligious professors, began to grow ashamed of admitting their faith. To spare themselves from ridicule for keeping the Church fasts, they boldly ate meat on Fridays. This class of self-styled progressives were to know that in their midst lived a few fearless Parisians who intended to exercise their free will and to assert their moral convictions without intimidation.

When Leo returned with his friends to the Hotel d'Angleterre, they went in search of Madame Contour to acquaint her with what had taken place.

Madame's face beamed while she listened. "You did that at the Maison de la Riche? Oh, Leo, your mother will be proud of you for doing this. And God will certainly reward you for your open profession of faith," she said, for she had long deplored the growing indifference of French Catholics.

"Why should we shy away from professing our faith? Daily our religion is ridiculed openly at the university and no one apologizes to us for making public jibes at the religious practices which as Catholics we must hold dear," Leo explained.

"But, Madame, don't you think perhaps Leo was a bit too outspoken when he told the waiter who was recommending pork, to keep the pigs in their pen?" asked Martin, one of Leo's three companions.

"Well, if either you or I made such remarks," parried Madame Contour, "we could not, as the saying goes, get away with it. But Mr. Dupont is so different. He seems to have been made to give utterance to words that carry truth to the very door of one's heart." She paused for a moment, and saw that Leo made no objection. "Besides, if the enemies of Christianity stop at nothing to openly ridicule Christianity, shall we stop at every turn to consult the book of etiquette lest we offer annoyance?"

"I guess not, but, frankly, from the threatening look Professor Albert gave us, he might have felt quite annoyed, to say the least. Do you suppose he'll demote us?" asked Martin again.

"Don't cross the bridge before you get there. Wait until you return to classes. One thing is sure. You have done nothing wrong, and therefore have nothing to worry about."

There were many others among the university students who spent the week-end speculating as to the possible effects Leo's little coup of Friday evening would have. They all knew Professor Albert's antireligious tendencies. They knew him as a veritable fanatic in opposition to everything connected with the Church, so much so that even the piously inclined Catholics in his class found themselves victims of his relentless propaganda and grew timid in the profession of their faith, lax in keeping the fasts or attending mass. A man of such deep-seated prejudices could be counted on to inflict a reprisal on Leo and his friends for their highly effective demonstration at the Maison de la Riche, mused the students.

When classes were resumed on Monday morning, and the students were seated at their desks, a tense feeling of apprehension filled the room. Professor Albert would presently open the door and enter, and soon enough they would learn his reaction. Catholic students who had dared to oppose the faculty's irreligious tendencies would soon learn to be cautious, they would soon learn to settle into a groove of passivity if they desired a measure of peace and well-being. Suddenly the door was thrust open! Leo and his three confreres nearly bounded out of their seats when instead of Professor Albert they saw a stranger enter the room.

"I am your new instructor," he announced pleasantly as he ascended the rostrum. "Certain unexpected changes have been made. Professor Albert has been appointed to teach another class."

With one sweeping gesture all eyes turned to look at Leo Dupont, who in turn had to try very hard not to appear more amazed than all the other students. With their eyes on him, their questioning glances seemed to speak louder than words: "Did you, Leo Dupont, know beforehand that Professor Albert would be changed? Is that why you dared to stage that religious demonstration in the dining room of the Maison de la Riche?"

But Leo's face turned stony in aspect. Let them think as they will. As for himself, Leo had an objective lesson which he now pondered in the depths of his heart—man had but to heed the voice of his conscience and act. God would do the rest!

Leo's three friends, however, who did not possess his deep spiritual discernment, already began secretly to nurse fears for the future. Professor Albert was not out of the way completely, they reflected. Next year they might be in his class and, knowing Professor Albert's vindictive tendencies, they felt indisposed to look forward to a cheerful future.

Leo, on the other hand, overflowing with gratitude for this unexpectedly happy turn of events, was unable to focus his attention on the lecture of the new professor. He was busy planning a further campaign. Every Friday night during the school term, Leo would muster a friend or two to go dining with him in fashionable restaurants and hotels in Paris, where, in clear, audible tones, fish and more fish would be ordered. Leo's campaign was not fruitless. Here and there students began to observe the Friday fasts. If the elegant and rich Leo Dupont was not ashamed of his religion, but took such pains to openly proclaim his convictions and to all appearances was none the worse for it socially, there did not seem much sense in catering to false human respect.

6

A slow drizzle fell through the long day. Leo, who liked rain when he was inside, did not relish its continuance into the evening when he was expected out. Still he was determined to keep his social engagement. He donned his high hat and white gloves, ready to face the storm outside, when he suddenly remembered to take with him a $500 note. The evening's affair was a charity ball, and guests would be expected to buy chances and bid for prizes. Hurriedly, he walked to the mahogany dresser where he usually kept large bills. Opening the top drawer, he peered into a small metal box but found it was empty. "Oh, well, I guess I must have placed it in the other compartment," he said to himself. But he soon learned it was not there either. He then opened a second drawer, and a third, but to no avail. He proceeded to search through the various pockets of his coats that hung in the wardrobe. Half an hour passed, and still Leo was trying to locate his note.

"Luke, go get Madame Contour. I don't know what happened to my money," he ordered his servant.

Luke ran to fetch Madame Contour. He observed that his master seemed to be in a mood bordering on real anger. Usually so obliging and even-tempered he was now greatly perturbed.

Madame Contour came hastily and helped to search for the missing note, but without success. Meanwhile Leo, who had been struggling within himself for some time, finally revealed his angry suspicions, "It's no use looking for something that has been stolen, Madame!" Leo's eyes flashed angrily, and Madame Contour turned pale.

Completely amazed, she asked, "Mr. Dupont, what are you saying? You have lived at this hotel nearly five years and never suffered any losses. Who would at this time steal your $500 note?"

"Who do you suppose? No one else but he, he stole my money!" exclaimed Leo, pointing an accusing finger at Luke. "No one else knows where I keep my money, and no one else has the key to my room except he . . . ."

Luke was stunned. If he turns me over to the police, he thought, I will most certainly be jailed. He had no way to defend himself. Overcome with fear, he looked up at Madame Contour, but she, noticing Leo's determination, did not intend to add to his annoyance by arguing with Leo or taking Luke's part.

Turning to Leo, she said as calmly as possible, "Mr. Dupont, you are distressed and in a hurry. You have an appointment and I know you are anxious to keep it and this incident has upset you. Therefore, I suggest you go at once to keep your appointment, for you are already late. As for the money, I shall gladly make you a loan of the $500 note, and I propose further that you leave me your key so I can search the room in your absence."

"Very well," said Leo, and then sauntered out of the room.

Left alone, Madame Contour made a thorough search for the missing note, which she finally found jammed in the rear of the top drawer, caught where it was entirely concealed from view. When Leo returned later that evening, she at once brought the note to him.

"Here is your note. It has been found!"

"Found? But where?"

"In the dresser where you had placed it. On taking out the top drawer, I found it jammed at the rear."

Leo's face fell. He looked at his servant and dropped to his knees. "I beg you to forgive the injustice I have done you. I am very sorry. How can I make it up to you?" Then, as if to himself, but still clearly and audibly, Leo added, "I have accused you of the greatest evil in the world, since I accused you of committing a mortal sin. And all the while you were innocent!"

Madame Contour stood motionless as she watched the handsome Leo Dupont, the young college student of Paris and brilliant aristocrat, actually kneel before his hired servant asking forgiveness. As long as she would live Madame Contour would remember this scene. She would recall it to others later on and stand witness to the admirable honesty of Leo Dupont on this occasion, as she would say, "We would wish to make a saint appear as one who never committed a fault, who never was guilty of a misjudgment, or who was never overcome by anger. Ah, such was not Mr. Leo Dupont! I don't believe saints ever were men without faults. What distinguishes true Christian greatness is one's capacity to admit his guilt and make restitution for an injustice, whether it be in the matter of restoring one's good name or his material goods."

Leo Dupont, the schoolboy at Martinique, was not flawless. With the other boys he joined in pranks and frivolity when he was told to study his lesson. But he was the only one of the group who had the candor to confess. Now, as a grown man, Leo, precipitated into a much greater wrong, did not hesitate to admit it and to ask openly for pardon.

Luke, confused and bewildered, did not know what to say or do. He remembered how often in his life he had accused others and misjudged them, but never had he thought of kneeling before anyone to ask forgiveness. And yet his wealthy and highly educated young master, casting human respect to the winds, kneeled before a servant to ask forgiveness of him. Surely it would suffice if the master, discovering his error of judgment, would say simply something to the effect that he was glad to learn the servant did not take the money. Another would have tapped the hired man on the shoulder, tossed him a five-frank note and, with an air of superiority, said, "Luke, here's a little tip as a compensation for my making a small error of judgment regarding you and my missing money. After all, you can't blame me for thinking you took the money since you're the only one who knows where I keep it. How was I to guess it got jammed at the rear of the drawer?" But no such false reasoning found its way into Leo's heart. He was never a hypocrite.

He did not pass off a serious matter lightly. Reasoning logically, he placed his finger directly on the sore spot even if the sore spot was right in his own heart, so that by doing this he could apply the remedy, no matter how painful to his human nature.

One week after the incident, Madame Contour met Leo in the lobby. "Luke has been showing me some of the presents you've given him to repay for that slight misjudgment," she said.

"It wasn't slight, Madame," replied Leo calmly.

"Well, at any rate, you've made it up to him a hundredfold," she said reassuringly. "Why, even Luke himself told me you really did him no harm. After all, you never told anyone except him and me about your suspicions. . . ."

"That was enough, and by far too much, to constitute a serious misdeed."

"By the way, you know what Luke asked me? He asked if it is not enough to go to confession and to admit one's faults. Should one also come to the person whom one has falsely accused and ask his forgiveness."

"And what did you answer him?"

"I told Luke I would ask you for the answer."

"Tell Luke that where property has been stolen or a good name injured there is no forgiveness for these sins in the confessional unless the stolen property is restored, or in the case of a good name dishonored, steps are taken to undo the harm. Now returning stolen goods is not so difficult. One need only to repay the sum with interest, and make the sacramental confession sincerely. But where the good name of another is injured, there arises a problem of greater dimensions. First, the injured party must be approached and forgiveness asked of him. Next, one must as much as lies in one's power contact all those persons outside who have learned of the calumny and who have been prejudiced against the wronged man. All should beware of accusing others more than they should guard against the worst of misfortunes . . . ."

Madame Contour listened to Leo with rapt attention.

"Don't credit me with eloquence, Madame. These are the

words of Father Frayssinous whom I had gone to see the morning after the unhappy episode. Father Frayssinous was greatly disappointed with me. He scolded me for a long time. I'll never forget it. 'Beware of rash judgments, Leo,' he said. 'If you dare to accuse an innocent man of evil, you are in great danger. Today you falsely blame perhaps only a servant. Tomorrow it will be a friend, an equal. And next year perhaps you will forget yourself so far as to impugn evil to God's anointed. When you do that you are on the road to perdition.' These, Madame, are the words of Father Frayssinous, who has been my confessor for nearly four years. I realize how right he is for I have a very fiery temper that I must curb. Father Frayssinous knows me well and he will not let me deceive myself, for which I am grateful. And all this makes me remember my mother's advice the night before I left home. She told me that God, the priest in the confessional, and I were the three most important factors in my life. How well I realize the truth of her words now!"

7

As Leo descended lower in his own self-esteem, he rose ever higher in the estimation of others, and also in the favor of God. People began to understand that when Leo Dupont was invited somewhere, invariably the conversation about worldly things would give way to some topic of religious or charitable interest. Moreover, since Leo's personality was so compelling and since his law studies developed his rare gift of eloquence, no one minded if Leo took the floor to expound spiritual verities.

"Every Frenchman is a Catholic," he would say, smiling, "so let's not beat around the bush. Let's talk about the really important things that matter." And then, before anyone realized it, Leo would be quoting Father Frayssinous, or Saint Thomas Aquinas, or his favorite Saint Martin, the miracle-worker of France. "Why not? Why, the very island on which I was born was named after Saint Martin—Martinique! Did you know that Saint Martin . . . ." and straightaway Leo would introduce his hearers to the amazing miracles performed by the outstanding thaumaturgist of France.

One evening at a social, an elderly lady, Madame Rivois, asked, "Mr. Dupont, do you by chance know where the Convent of the Mesdames of the Sacred Heart is located?"

"Yes, the convent is on Varenne Street."

"Do you know the superioress there?"

"You mean Madame Sophie Barat, the foundress?" asked Leo.

"Yes."

"I know her only by name, Madame, which is mentioned in Paris quite frequently. She is undoubtedly a religious of great learning and spirituality," answered Leo with a note of reverence.

"Well, for the moment it is not her spirituality that I intend to discuss. It is to settle a very material affair that I introduced this conversation about Madame Barat. Leo I want you to pay a visit to Madame Barat!"

"May I ask what for?"

"To put it bluntly, it is to settle a certain embarrassing financial matter, an unpaid bill at Madame's boarding school. It's this way. Two young ladies, sisters, the Mesdemoiselles LeRoux, both attended Madame Barat's school. The parents of these two girls through some turn of events have become financially unable to meet the indebtedness for their daughters' school and board. It is, of course, a delicate matter and a bit embarrassing to the LeRoux, as to their friends who, therefore, hesitate to negotiate directly with Madame Barat. But you, being a stranger, can certainly pay her a visit to ask her to make an allowance on the unpaid bill, or to cancel it."

"But I don't understand. Do you expect me to approach Madame Barat, whom I have never met, and to make demands on her charity in behalf of people I don't know?"

"Well, Leo, there's nothing wrong in your going. You have such a reputation for charity, that, well . . . ."

"The compliment is undeserved, Madame. I am far from being a philanthropist," offered Leo. He thrust his hands into his pockets and stared aimlessly out the window.

"Leo, really, I meant no offense, for you know I am an old woman and a friend of your mother. All I meant to ask was for you to speak a few words with Madame Barat in behalf of the LeRoux family. It would be an act of charity!"

"Charity? Hardly! I am inclined to hold that contributions to the Church, to religious, to priests and nuns are correctly called acts of charity. Now you are sending me to a convent to demand that the superioress make a contribution to lay people by canceling a just debt, and you call that an act of charity on my part. I call it extortion!" Leo paused for a moment and then added, "Madame, I am unaccustomed to such missions. It seems highly improper to accost a nun to ask her to make concessions on an altogether just boarding-school bill . . . ."

Nothing more was said during the remainder of the evening, but when the guests began taking their leave, Leo approached Madame Rivois and said simply, "I've changed my mind. I'll go to see Madame Barat about that unpaid bill tomorrow morning."

Early the next day, Leo went to the convent of the Mesdames of the Sacred Heart where he asked to see Madame Barat personally. The discussion that ensued was exactly what Leo had expected.

Madame Barat explained her position without mincing words. "Mr. Dupont, we are sorry that the LeRoux family are financially embarrassed, but they must also understand that we sisters here have to meet our expenses. The nuns, through their vow of poverty, have relinquished all right to worldly goods, and their object in life now is to impart a Catholic education to our young French ladies. But the convent and school must be kept up and this calls for financial resources. We must insist that bills for board and tuition be met. We likewise must meet our bills for food, for fuel, for linens, and all other necessities in connection with conducting a boarding school. Surely, no one can expect poor nuns to supply students with food and board free of charge."

Leo fully agreed with the wisdom of Madame Barat's words.

"Tell me, Mr. Dupont, don't you think that when the parents of the LeRoux girls recognized their inability to pay for their daughters' stay here, they should have at once withdrawn their children from this school?"

"Yes, Sister, I do," conceded Leo. "It wasn't fair for the parents to continue to keep two grown daughters at this boarding school when they had met with reverses and saw they could not afford to meet the bill for such expenditures." Leo paused and then asked, "How much do they owe you, Madame?"

Madame Barat brought the register of accounts and began calling out the accounts. Finally she said, "Then there is an extra bill for music, for piano lessons, and for singing for both girls."

"Piano and singing lessons when they knew they could not afford to pay even for their board and ordinary tuition? I can understand your feelings, Madame Barat, and I see clearly why you cannot let the bill go. It seems like taking undue advantage."

Madame Barat grew pensive. How much money did it require to outfit the boarding school, how much effort to beg and plead for donations, to save extra dollars by doing the laundry and the cooking in addition to the tedious hours of teaching school, to teach music and art. And then the Le-Roux kept two daughters in the institution exacting every service and facility, and at the end of the school term they perfunctorily informed the superioress that they would not pay their bill because they had financial reverses.

"Whether you pay or whether you will not pay," Madame Barat had told them, "that is your affair. But you owe this bill."

"Sister," said Leo, "this is my last year in Paris, for I shall complete my law studies here in the spring. I have somewhat of a balance left over from my annual allowance, which is considerable. If you will accept my offer, I shall be happy to pay this bill."

"You are very generous, sir, but why should you be the one to assume this obligation?" asked Madame Barat, confused for the moment.

"Sister, I do it for you. I understand that so long as this bill remains unpaid you and the institution of which you are superioress are made to suffer. When institutions like yours suffer, Sister, then it is the Church that suffers. No one can fail to see that!"

Madame Barat gratefully accepted the magnanimous charity of her young visitor, but only when he agreed to accept a reduction on the bill, which she suggested.

"Now, only one more favor," said Leo in a hushed voice. "Please, not a word of this to anyone," he begged, and the nun promised to keep his charity a secret.

When Leo finally left the convent, snow was falling fast,

piling itself high here and there, but his mind was not on the sudden change of weather. He was thinking of Madame Barat. Nor would he ever forget the sense of justice which permeated everything she had said, however much the undisciplined amateur in Christian asceticism would wish to spread the idea that saints were "easy," that they quickly and unhesitatingly canceled bills due them, gesturing nonchalantly as they said, "Why, never mind, everything is all right, just forget it."

Leo knew that real saints harbored no such irresponsibility. The saints were conscientious, they were just and consequently deeply imbued with the importance of attending carefully to all money matters. The belongings and earnings of the Convent of the Sacred Heart were not the property of Madame Barat which she could dispose of according to her personal likes. The convent with its belongings was not the private property of any of the nuns. It was there as a means of carrying on the work of the Church. The income of the convent had, therefore, to be administered with prudence, and every dollar accounted for with accuracy.

Madame Barat, who after her death was canonized a saint, had given Leo Dupont on that winter day an admirable object lesson in the cardinal virtue of justice as it pertained to money matters and unpaid bills, and Leo was never to forget it.

8

It was still early in February and the weather whipped everyone outdoors into a brisk step, making every passerby on the Rue de la Colombier pull up his collar and thrust his hands deep into his pockets. Although there was still snow on the ground from the previous night's steady fall when Leo came down about nine that morning, the snow clouds were dispersing and here and there a patch of blue appeared through rows of Parisian houses.

"Clement, take me straight to the stationery store on the Rue de la Campagne. I'm all out of supplies," Leo said to his jockey who alighted from the tilbury where he waited in front of the Hotel d'Angleterr

"You wants to go to Mr. Bordeaux's stationery 'stablishment?" asked Clement with noticeable accent on the last word, which due to associating with so educated a gentleman as Mr. Leo Dupont he had recently added to his vocabulary and which he could not avoid using whenever the opportunity presented itself.

"Yes, to Mr. Bordeaux's, Clement. You know very well that there is no other stationer on the Rue de la Campagne," answered Leo, slightly vexed. He had several important matters on his mind, chief of which were the spring examinations which he must pass to be admitted to the bar. Those examinations were all coming up within a month. After five years of study in Paris he should have his law degree. He therefore resolved to apply himself wholeheartedly to study during the intervening weeks. To carry out his resolution it was necessary to first put his notes and briefs into proper order, and for this he needed a generous supply of writing materials.

When Leo entered the store on the Rue de la Campagne, he noticed a group of five men with anxious faces speaking earnestly with the proprietor, Mr. Bordeaux, who seemed greatly worried. Recognizing one of the long-faced gentlemen as the bookseller whom he had patronized for many years, Leo approached him. "Good morning, Mr. Vrayet. How have you been?"

"Just fine, and how are you, Mr. Dupont?" He tried to sound cheerful but his effort fell short.

Leo then stepped forward and extended his hand to the proprietor over the counter. "You seem worried, Mr. Bordeaux. I hope there is nothing seriously wrong."

"Well, yes, there is, Mr. Dupont," said the proprietor slowly. "These gentlemen are my creditors," he confessed. "I owe them money and am not able to pay. They came here in a body to decide what steps to take against me."

Leo looked at the group now beginning to move about uneasily, as if embarrassed.

Mr. Bordeaux went on, "Of course, Mr. Dupont, it is true I do owe them money and I do not deny that they have a right to demand what is theirs. It is, moreover, quite a large sum that I owe—$300, a sum so large for me to repay at this time that it is altogether out of the question for me to settle the debt."

"But, Mr. Bordeaux, how did you ever get into arrears for such a large sum of money? I thought you were a good businessman, a hustler in your work, a man who got on well."

"I did, Mr. Dupont, until four months ago when the calamities of Job were heaped upon me." Mr. Bordeaux had not been a stationer for twenty years without availing himself of the advantages that accrued to those who habitually associated with students, lawyers, writers, and clerics; each in turn left traces of a particular kind on the vocabulary of the stationery proprietor. And, in truth, the scriptural Job *did* bear a resemblance now to the distracted stationer on this occasion as he began to recount to Leo a series of doleful misfortunes. "It all began when I had a fire that destroyed $500 worth of my best stock. Next, I took seriously ill and was confined in a hospital for three weeks. During this long period, my store had to remain closed. No money coming in and expenses piling up just the same—rent, heat, food for my family, and a hospital bill besides. Just as I began to recover, my wife was struck down with pneumonia. I had to take her to the hospital, and then my three children, poorly cared for during all this illness, each in turn contracted serious colds—and so it has been since the winter weather set in last November."

"That is too bad," said Leo, and all five creditors repeated in sad monotone, "Yes, it is too bad."

Leo looked sympathetically at Mr. Bordeaux and asked, "And how are your wife and your children now?"

"Thank God, they are all out of danger and getting stronger each day, and that's why I say that, being able to work once more, I know I'll get ahead and everything will be all right in due time. But I don't have $300 to pay these men now. I even owe the baker and the butcher!" The stationer looked up, offering a suggestion, "Now, I know I shall be able to pay in the future, that is, if I am given time to get ahead, let us say about six months . . . ." With this proposal made, the stationer waited for the worst.

Seeing that the creditors continued to stare at the floor, silent as stone and as immovable, Leo looked to Mr. Vrayet and asked, "Well, Mr. Vrayet, what do you say to waiting?"

"Waiting six months? Oh, no, we have already waited four months. Six months is too long to wait, and besides, there's no assurance he can pay the money even in two years!"

Leo stepped back a few paces and then turned a serious face to the group who now looked up at him a bit frightened, nonplused, or vexed, he did not know which. "Gentlemen, $300 is due you from Mr. Bordeaux for four months, which debt he does not deny. What do you propose to do in this matter, since you declare that you will not wait?"

"There is nothing left for us to do but to take over Mr. Bordeaux's business, sell it for what it is worth and settle our claims!"

At this, something happened to Leo which seemed to hurl him in one jump to the rostrum of a courtroom. He was no longer only a law student preparing for the bar. He became suddenly a full-fledged lawyer, eloquently pleading for clemency in behalf of his defendent who stood there behind the counter, pale and trembling.

"Gentlemen, I beg you to consider what will become of this poor stationer if you should have recourse to the drastic measure of selling his business to satisfy your claims. This man has himself, his wife and children to support. He has, moreover, patronized your firms for years and paid you large sums of money for the goods he purchased. Now, for the first time in his life, he meets with reverses such as can befall any of you five, and you, disregarding everything, are pressing a case of insolvency which will overnight make a pauper of a respectable citizen. Mr. Bordeaux is not a slothful, irresponsible man who spends his time in idleness. His present inability to settle this debt cannot be imputed to him as a crime nor even a fault. Mr. Bordeaux, moreover, is no drunkard, no fly-by-night agent of illegal enterprises who, through deceit, is trying to rob you! A fire and sickness overwhelmed Mr. Bordeaux, gentlemen, and these misfortunes could also at any time happen to you, as they did to him. Year after year, this dutiful stationer stands behind that counter waiting and serving customers six days out of the week, spring, summer, winter, and fall. He enjoys the respect of his wife and his children as well as the community, and you would mercilessly see his business dissolved, see him bankrupt and open to every danger of body and soul—and why? To pay your bills of $300, which divided among five of you creditors is less than $100 each. Yes, to see your claims settled safely in your pockets without any delay whatsoever, you refuse to wait, to extend this honest merchant sufficient time to get back on his feet."

The five creditors shifted nervously. Vrayet, who knew Leo and prided himself on saying the young aristocrat from Martinique was a good friend of his, whispered a frail "Well, I'll agree to wait a while longer for what is due me, Mr. Dupont."

Leo was disgusted with the heartlessness and lack of enthusiasm that echoed from the weak offer of Mr. Vrayet. And when he saw that despite his appeal the other four made no comment at all, Leo realized that his pleading must give way to something more effective. If he wished to see Mr. Bordeaux retain his business, he had better stop wasting time.

Leo realized, of course, that he spent each year's allowance as it came along, and now remembering that he had drawn considerably on his resources to settle someone's unpaid bill at the Convent of the Sacred Heart only last month, he knew he could not possibly afford to give away any more money. He still had four months of school ahead of him and what money he had left would be barely enough to take care of his personal needs. Yet he must find some way to meet this situation, he told himself, as he began pacing the floor, keeping time with the pendulum of the huge clock that ticked away the fleeting seconds. Then suddenly looking up, Leo noticed something through the window of the store which gave him an idea. With long swift strides he walked toward the front of the shop; something in his manner made all five creditors turn their eyes upon him. With a sweeping gesture, he flung open the door.

"Gentlemen, do you see that horse and tilbury? They are mine! Take them and sell them! They may not bring enough to cover the entire debt but they should bring at least $200 and this should satisfy you until Mr. Bordeaux can pay the rest."

A cold blast blew in through the door which added to the discomfort of the group who shamefacedly blinked at Leo. Leo walked up to Mr. Bordeaux to settle the matter with legal formality.

"Mr. Bordeaux, if you will give me a blank bill of sale, I shall make over my vehicle and horse to you so you can settle the indebtedness for which these Christian gentlemen have assembled here to press you."

"But, Mr. Dupont, you're accustomed to your vehicle, I mean, you'll be lost without it in Paris, sir," began Mr. Bordeaux.

"I have a carriage and a pair of horses besides the tilbury

I am making over to you. Since I expect to leave Paris shortly, I ought to begin disposing of some of my excess cargo," Leo answered smiling.

"But, Mr. Dupont, you can't do that. I know this horse and tilbury mean a lot to you. I remember the day you got them you were bursting with joy."

Leo smiled at the recollection. What Parisian gentleman of good taste wouldn't be bursting with pride to have one vehicle for the daytime and another for the more formal occasions of evening or Sunday afternoon? To part with the tilbury four months before leaving Paris was costing Leo a generous amount of self-denial, but Leo felt he had no choice. He had pleaded with five men to respond to a call on their charity, but they had refused.

Mr. Bordeaux wanted to protest further, at least to make a few more of the polite overtures a man in his position was expected to make in embarrassing situations, but Leo's determined look stopped him. It was no use. There was no room for sham in the presence of a man like Leo. "May God reward you, Mr. Dupont," was all he could manage to say. Tears welled in his eyes as he walked to the steel cabinet from which he drew out a large legal form. He handed it to Leo who filled in the dotted lines that legally turned over the horse and tilbury to the distracted Mr. Bordeaux. The embarrassed creditors slyly walked to the opposite end of the store to spare themselves from being witness to an act of spontaneous goodness on the part of a very unusual young man.

Leo quietly walked out of the store "Get down, Clement," he said, "we're walking."

"What's that yer sayin', Mr. Leo?" asked the amazed jockey.

"I said get down. And don't take all morning."

"But what about the tilbury? Mr. Leo, I can't leave the horse and tilbury here!"

"Yes, you can. We don't own the horse and tilbury any longer."

"Don't own the tilbury no more? Land sakes, Mr. Leo!" cried the jockey, "done you gone and gambled yer fine horse and tilbury?" Clement was not an ex-street-sweeper for nothing. In his vivid mind the turn of a pair of dice or the shuffling of a deck of cards on a darkened street corner or in an alley were realities not to be forgotten. True, he had never heard anything about Mr. Leo to lead him to think his master ever threw dice or played cards for stakes, but what was this thing about not owning the tilbury any longer? "Get down, Clement, the horse and tilbury don't belong to us any longer . . . ." It could mean only one thing to Clement. Mr. Leo done met some friends in the stationery place and there was a game, yes, and Mr. Leo done lost! Slowly the jockey began to climb down from his high seat in the cherished tilbury, dragging himself disconsolately to catch up with his master, who was already a hundred yards ahead.

"What was it you were asking me back there, Clement?" questioned Leo when he saw the jockey at his side.

"I asked you, Mr. Leo, done you gone and gambled fer the horse and tilbury?"

"Oh, gambled for it? Yes, in a certain way, Clement, that's what I did. I gambled for it," Leo answered, amused. "Only it was a sure sort of gamble, Clement, the kind in which the one who loses something here below gains something up above."

The jockey scratched his head. Mr. Leo's puzzles were lately upsetting his equilibrium. Those high law studies of the master were just too much for him. Half the time Clement didn't know what Mr. Leo was even talking about.

"Can I carry yer bundle fer you, Mr. Leo?" Clement asked respectfully enough, but his mind was not on the bundle. As he trudged along, he kept looking back longingly at the deserted tilbury and horse, of which he had grown very fond. Clement and his master walking in the snow, while the tilbury stood vacant and abandoned! The queerest things can happen to people, thought the jockey silently to himself.

9

LEO AND his jockey were turning in on the Rue de la Colombier when someone called out to them from behind. "Well, fancy catching Leo Dupont walking in the snow!"

Leo turned around and, recognizing a classmate said, smiling, "Oh, it's you, Charles! How have you been?"

"Just fine! But tell me, Leo, where's your cabriolet or your tilbury? How is it you are walking?"

"I left my carriage in the stable," answered Leo evasively, hoping Charles would not press him further about the tilbury, for he had no intention of explaining to anyone how he came to part with it. Quickly changing the subject, Leo asked, "When are examinations, do you know, Charles?"

"Some time next month, but I don't know the exact dates. Are you cramming, Leo?"

"Who isn't? I guess the examinations will be rather tough."

"I don't think so. If you have enough attendance certificates I understand you're safely through."

"Did you say attendance certificates?" Leo asked, surprised.

"That's right. Professor Durant is a stickler for attendance. No student will be allowed so much as to take one examination until he first secures signed certificates from him as to attendance at lectures."

"That will make it tough for me!"

"Why, Leo?"

"Don't you know? I'm never at public lectures any more. I quit attending altogether," answered Leo.

"But since when, old man?"

"Since last fall," he replied.

"What made you quit the lectures? Did you expect to become a lawyer without going to school?" said Charles ironically.

"Don't be funny. I enrolled under a private tutor. The university professors with their continuous jibes at religion were too much for me." Meanwhile the wind kept blowing fiercely from the corner, so Leo added, "But I can't hold you here to talk about my troubles in this cold. Thanks for the information. I'll go up to see Professor Durant without delay."

"When you go be sure you think up a good alibi!"

"What do you mean?" asked Leo, puzzled.

"Just this. If you expect to make the professor believe you were at classes when you weren't there at all, you'd better make up a story that will sound convincing."

"Hold on, Charles. Do you think I'm going to see Professor Durant with the intention of deceiving him about my attendance?"

"What else? You want your certificates signed, don't you?"

"Yes, but I don't intend to lie in order to get them!" Leo turned on his heels. He was indignant. For five years he had known Charles at school. Now, on the eve of graduation, Charles had no better opinion of him than to judge him an ordinary cheat.

When Leo reached his hotel, his jockey, still brooding over the abandoned tilbury, was anxious to get some definite instructions about the carriage.

"Mr. Leo, do you wants me to bring the carriage and horses around this afternoon?" he asked.

"Yes, Clement, by all means. Call for me with the carriage at three o'clock. We are going to call on Professor Durant."

John, the doorman, was visibly puzzled when he saw the aristocratic Leo walking up the driveway with the disconsolate jockey trailing behind.

Taking Clement aside, John asked him pointedly, "What happened to the horse and tilbury?"

"I really dunno!" answered Clement.

"You don't know?"

"Well, Mr. Leo said it was a case of losin' somethin' down

here for to gain somethin' up there!" Clement's fingers pointed below and then above, as he spoke.

"Losing the horse and tilbury! Man, are you crazy?" John did not like being left in suspense. "How can anybody lose a horse and tilbury?"

"I couldn't rightly explain that to ye, John. Facts is, I don't know no more but what I sawed and heard which ain't sufficient enuff fer me to comprehend."

"Sufficient to comprehend! Stop showin' off with big words you copy from Mr. Leo, and hurry up and tell me where did you lose the horse and tilbury, Clement?"

"In front of the stationery store. Right by the curb!"

"Well, if you know where it is why don't you go on and get it?"

"Because Mr. Leo done said the tilbury don't belongs to us no mo, nohow!"

"Don't belong?"

"Yeah, that's what he said. We walked home all the way."

"Land sakes!" exclaimed John. "What's happening to Mr. Leo?"

"I dunno, but believe me I'm hopin' he ain't settin' hisself to losing his carriage next, coz I'll be out of a job. I'm really only half of a jockey now that the tilbury's gone."

At half past three that same afternoon, Leo was walking down the long corridor of the faculty hall in search of Professor Durant. A tall man with austere features passed him in the corridor, but Leo decided to consult the porter for information.

"Can you direct me to Professor Durant's quarters?"

"Yes, sir, that was Professor Durant who just passed you down the hall. He turned in at Room 63. That's where you'll find him now."

To a quiet tap on his door, the professor replied with a monotonous, "Come in."

"Professor Durant, I am a law student in my last year and I have come to inquire about getting my certificates signed," Leo said, coming straight to the point.

How has your attendance been?" asked the professor. "Have you come regularly to my lectures?"

"No, sir, I have not attended your lectures at all. In fact, this is the first time that I have had the pleasure of meeting you. That was the reason why I did not recognize you when I passed you by in the corridor a few moments ago."

The professor looked at the student before him a trifle bewilderedly, but said nothing.

"You see, Professor," Leo went on, "I have been studying under a private tutor. That is the reason I never attend public lectures."

The professor asked Leo to be seated and began to question him about French statutes. Leo showed himself well prepared. Moreover, his delivery was correct and his choice of words precise; he had a natural eloquence that impressed Professor Durant.

"I suggest that you come to my lectures two or three times between now and the end of school and I shall sign your certificates which will qualify you to take the examinations."

"Thank you, Professor," answered Leo politely. "I shall do as you say."

Professor Durant, pausing with Leo at the door, could not refrain from a few remarks. "Young man, you have an admirable trait which should make you a good lawyer. You have the rare quality of honesty. Believe me, I have taught law for many years but this is the first time I have been approached by a student with such complete frankness. I have had the sad experience of interviewing students who come here deliberately deceiving me as to their attendance, in order to get their certificates signed. 'Ah, Professor,' one told me this morning, 'but I have attended ever so many lectures in your hall.' To this I objected, saying, 'If you have attended, how is it I do not recognize you at all?' What do you suppose he told me then? 'Oh, Professor,' he exclaimed, 'I can explain why you failed to notice me in class. You see I always select a desk behind a pillar which practically conceals me from view!' Now, there are no pillars in my lecture hall," the professor said and then shook his head. "I am in a dilemma when I try to fathom what sort of lawyers these students will turn out to be. They are already young criminals with deceit in their hearts. How will they ever become the champions of the oppressed who seek and thirst after justice?"

"But, Professor Durant, you speak as a believer! The words you just said are from the gospels. This is the first time I have heard a Parisian professor . . . ."

"Yes, I know what you are about to say and I am not surprised. I, too, was once one of those who, under the guise of false intellectualism, thought it opportune to disclaim religion and to deny a future life!"

"And now?" asked Leo, hanging on the professor's every word. .

"Now I am repentant. I regret the day I became so confused and blundering as to proclaim in defense of materialism against religion. I have since learned that there is no motive for speaking the truth or defending justice, which is the realm of the lawyer, if there be no God. You might as well ask a blind man to describe for you the colors of the spectrum as to expect an unbelieving man who denies a life hereafter to tell the truth, to defend justice, or to keep within the law. There is no reason at all for keeping spiritual obligations such as these if there be no spiritual life. Cheat, lie, steal, deceive, take what you can and scream out to the world that you have it all coming to you! Such is the conduct that must follow upon the premise that there is no God. I shudder to think what the world would become if the materialist should become its master. Order, decency, honesty — these things must disappear from the face of the earth if there be no belief in God; there is no motive for goodness and truth if there be no faith in God. When the freethinkers of France will return to God, then will order follow as day follows night."

In due time, Professor Durant signed the requisite certificates and Leo took the bar examinations and passed with excellent grades. He was now a lawyer. When commencement exercises were finished and Leo returned to his apartment at the Hotel d'Angleterre, he took his diploma and scrutinized it carefully, observed every solemn word of recommendation engraved on the expensive parchment, and then slowly and deliberately tossed it on the desk. He was experiencing his first genuine misgiving: "I wonder if I'll ever have any use for that diploma," he asked himself, and realized that it was imperative for him to decide that question now while he was in Paris, before returning home to Martinique. He was twenty-four years old. It was high time to decide one way or another what his future would be.

10

Two DAYS after graduation, Leo Dupont dressed in a plain black suit and tie. The customary fresh flower was missing from his lapel despite the fact that it was spring and Paris was enjoying the heights of fashion. He had not slept well and Madame Contour, who noticed him as he crossed the lobby, thought he looked years older. He seemed preoccupied and the smile that usually beamed from his face had given way to lips drawn in a straight line.

"Clement isn't here, sir," said John when he saw Leo dressed for the outdoors.

"I didn't expect him. I told him I wouldn't need him this morning."

"Shall I call you a cab?"

"Not today. I'll catch the public conveyance on the corner," said Leo in a matter-of-fact way.

"The common street-vehicle?" asked John, amazed.

Leo smiled to him without stopping to answer. And John, bewildered, kept staring until Leo disappeared from sight. Dressed all in black, no bouttoniere, no cane, no cab, and a felt hat in the spring! Mr. Leo was certainly losing his style, thought the doorman, wondering what had caused the change.

When at last Leo boarded the street car, he soon found how congested it was; with fat men pushing, and scullery maids hurrying off to work with large bundles under their arms. It was a salutary act of penance to bear on an occasion like this, Leo told himself as he rode on through the streets of Paris toward his destination. Besides, it was simply unthinkable for him to travel in his customary fine carriage drawn by a pair of well-groomed horses, considering the particular errand on which he was going. There ought to be a seemliness about all human conduct, Leo thought, and his destination today demanded a definite curtailment of worldly elegance. Leo was on his way to keep an appointment at the Sulpician Seminary.

"Is Father Lemarie in?" Leo asked the brother who opened the door.

"I expect you are Mr. Dupont?"

"I am," replied Leo.

"Then this way, please. Father Lemarie is expecting you. He told me to ask you to come to his office."

Leo was impressed by the atmosphere of the religious institution as he walked quietly down the corridor, by the bare walls, the silence, and the asceticism that pervaded every nook and corner. But, when a few moments later he came face to face with the novice-master, Father Lemarie, he knew that he could open his heart to him in all frankness.

"Now, my son, tell me what can I do for you," said the priest, losing no time in coming to the point.

"I came for advice, Father. I think I would like to be a priest."

The novice-master looked at his visitor earnestly and then said, "Well, my son, suppose you first tell me more about yourself. Tell me a little of your family background, your schooling, and your pursuits up till now. Were you born in Paris?"

"No, Father. I was born in Martinique," Leo began, and then went on to tell of his home in the colony. "I came to Paris five years ago to study for the bar. I graduated two days ago."

"So you are a lawyer now," said the novice-master approvingly. "And where did you attend school?" he asked.

Leo went on to tell the priest about his courses at the university, his acquaintance with Mr. Bordier, and his enrollment in the Society of Mary. "But I would not have you think that I am inclined to be a recluse, Father. To be frank, I rather enjoyed going to dances and balls, mixing with fashionable society and wearing fine clothes. I understand, of course, that being a priest would necessitate my giving all this up, but I am quite certain that I could do it."

Father Lemarie listened attentively. He was a member of the famed Society of St. Sulpice whose lifework was to lead and train young men for the priesthood. Not theirs to teach the ignorant, to baptize the infant, to do parish work, to go to foreign missions, or to evangelize the pagan. Not theirs to sanctify themselves and to win graces for others by a life of penance and prayer in the fastness of some solitary cloister. Theirs was an altogether different vocation. The Sulpician was a priest who dedicated his life to the training of other priests.

On that warm spring day in Paris, Leo had come to the right place in search of settling the problem of his vocation. If he really had the call to the priesthood, which he now deeply felt he had, then the Sulpicians would certainly help him to realize it.

Never did he feel such a strong desire to give up the whole world in order to become a seminarian as when a neat young man in a black cassock, having quietly knocked on the door, entered to address the novice-master, "Father, you told me to let you know when it was time for the final retreat conference. It is quarter to five now."

The novice-master nodded and the young man, smiling encouragingly to Leo, walked away.

"One of the seminarians?" asked Leo, unable to repress his interest.

"Not only a seminarian! That was a deacon."

"A deacon?"

"Yes. A deacon, you see, is a seminarian who has received Major Orders."

"Then this young man, this deacon, will soon be ordained?" asked Leo anxiously.

"Yes. In fact, he is one of a class of fifty who will be ordained at Notre Dame Cathedral tomorrow morning." Father Lemarie rose from his chair. "That is why I must now terminate this pleasant visit. I am due in the chapel at five to give the final conference of the retreat which ends tonight."

"Then I must not detain you another moment, Father," said Leo and he rose at once to leave.

"Son, I have a suggestion. Would you like to go to Notre Dame tomorrow to attend the ordination rites?"

"Oh yes, yes, I would, Father."

"Then I will ask the brother to give you a special ticket which will entitle you to a front pew." The priest smiled. and Leo could hardly contain his joy.

Father Lemarie left his visitor and proceeded to the chapel where the retreatants were already assembled. Leo, after waiting a while in the reception room, was handed an admission ticket which he enthusiastically deposited in his wallet and then walked outside, full of vibrant anticipation. The Sulpicians were wonderful, he told himself. How vapid the world, how vain everything on earth compared to the incomparably high station of the priesthood! Leo made quick resolution, he was offering everything he had to God, to the Master Whom he was determined to follow all the way. The environment of the Sulpician Seminary he had just visited seemed to inspire Leo with a spirit of self-denial he never expected would have been possible for him.

At Notre Dame the next day, Leo felt himself carried away as the organ sounded its first solemn strains and the blazing light from myriads of wax candles transformed the sanctuary into a place of exquisite beauty. As Leo looked at the white forms of deacons prostrated on the sanctuary floor, he began to think of himself as one of them some day. The pontifical ceremony progressed, and from his point of vantage, Leo, able to observe every move, felt ever greater fervor and devotion. Although the rites were long, he felt no fatigue. His eyes remained fixed on the altar and on the deacons. How long Leo continued absorbed in the holy drama he could never remember.

Suddenly something caught Leo's attention. Something the Bishop was doing made his blood run cold. He lost all rapture as he watched the Bishop anointing the hands of each ordinandus with holy chrism. First the thumb and index finger of each hand, then a cross on the palm. Leo needed no words to tell him what this meant. Slowly, deliberately, he turned his eyes away from the sanctuary. Mechanically, he now unfolded his hands and stared at his own thumb, the stub of something which had once in childhood resembled a thumb — but which was now deformed. Rapidly his mind went back many years as he saw himself at Chissay during a carefree summer vacation. As clearly as if he were there again in person, Leo saw the huge iron gate and Alfred his cousin perched upon it. He saw Alfred swinging violently, back and forth. Leo now became insensible to everything else except Alfred riding through that gateway with great force and crushing his thumb. It was not a dream. Leo's hand and the maimed thumb at which he now gazed with cold realism shattered all his hopes of a moment ago.

Tears streamed down Leo's face as he looked up again and continued to watch the bishop as he went on with the ceremony. Inwardly, Leo was drawing his own conclusions. The anointed hands of the priest were destined to hold the Body of Jesus Christ, true God and true Man, under the species of bread and wine. To be a priest, a man had to be whole. *Leo was not whole.* His hand was deformed. A freak accident in childhood had robbed him of his thumb. Why, oh, why did it all have to happen out there on his uncle's estate at Chissay that summer? Were it not for his deformed thumb he could hope to become a priest; the maimed hand would surely count him out!

But what about exceptions, what about seeking a dispensation? This thought of consolation came to assuage his temporary grief. It was only the angel in the Garden of Olives strengthening the agonizing Christ to drink to the bitterest dregs the cup of Calvary that still awaited a grim fulfillment. Leo knew there was no hope of delivery, only the hope of strength to carry the blow through without fainting on the way. And like the agonizing Christ, Leo kneeling there at Notre Dame came forth with an heroic, "Not my will, Father, but Thine be done!"

At the appointed hour on Monday evening, Leo was again at the Sulpician monastery to keep an appointment. When he was alone with Father Lemarie and the door of the small rear parlor was closed, Leo looked straight into the pale blue eyes of the novice-master. "Father, you don't have to worry. I believe I can take it," he managed, but when the words were finished tears welled in Leo's eyes.

For a few moments neither spoke. It would be difficult to estimate whose sorrow was keener. The priest remained speechless.

Leo was the one to break the silence for the second time, "I realized during the ceremony of the anointing of the hands with chrism that my deformed thumb constituted a serious impediment to my ever being ordained a priest."

"Son," finally came from Father Lemarie. He could say no more.

"But, Father, when I was here to see you Friday, it never even occurred to me that you had noticed my deformed thumb." Leo tried to sound like himself.

"Leo, we Sulpicians are trained to the task of observing everything in those who come here aspiring to be the future priests of God."

"Father, could a dispensation of some kind be secured in a particular case where there is some slight physical impediment?" Then without waiting for an answer, he added, "Of course, not that I, personally, would seek a dispensation. Besides, I thought it over all day yesterday and I said to myself again and again as I looked at my thumb, 'Leo, the perfect humanity of our Lord deserves to be handled with fingers which have their proper natural form. Even in the old law, the lamb which was selected for sacrifice was required to be without blemish of any kind. And now in the New Law, the hands of the priest which are destined to hold the sacred Body of Our Lord immolated on the altar ought also to be without any physical flaw. My hands do not answer that description.' "

The novice-master sympathetically invited Leo to sit down and to spend the afternoon with him. His class of deacons were now ordained priests, and he for the time being was without a particular charge. In the fall every Sulpician would again be assigned his particular duty, but summer was a time of rest, without definite responsibility, the priest told Leo.

It was no use for Leo to attempt to shift the conversation

to any other subject except that of the priesthood which had seemed to be in the palm of his hand, as it were, but was suddenly wrested from that hand because of a deformed thumb.

"Since attending last Saturday's services at Notre Dame, Father, I am a different person. It seemed to me that I was ready to grasp and to enfold to my bosom the most desirable object in all the world, but that object has suddenly been taken away from me. I try one way and then another to see if I can trace God's plan through this difficult pattern."

"And have you succeeded in any way to trace it?" asked the priest, studying Leo closely.

"Perhaps I have. As I see it, Father, if God had called me to be a priest He would have protected me from the accident that crippled my thumb, don't you think so?"

"Go ahead, Leo," encouraged the priest, nodding his head. "I think you are capable of tracing the whole pattern."

"No, Father, I would rather you did it for me. You see, when I try to figure it out for myself, I reach conclusions that seem close to presumptuous."

"For example?"

"Well, I've been thinking, for instance, about the one thing a Catholic should desire above everything else in this world. It is not necessarily to be a priest, or a brother, important as these vocations are. Rather, I concluded that the one goal should be, well . . . ." Leo hesitated.

"Go ahead, my son. What is that one goal every Catholic should strive after?" the priest pressed.

"To become a saint!" It was out. Leo shrank back into himself and then looked up at Father Lemarie inquiringly.

"And, my son, you think that it is presumptuous to have such thoughts?"

"Well, who am I, but one of millions in the world, with no works of penance or self-abnegation to my credit. I just began wondering if perhaps these thoughts bordered on pride."

"No, Leo, never! Disappointed in your desire to enter the priesthood, you looked into your soul to find the will of God in your regard. You found it. The call to sanctity, Leo, and not according to the way you would like to plan it, but according to the Divine Pattern. Obediently, without bitterness, you are conforming to God's designs. You do not protest against your misfortune. Rather, you have learned from it a great lesson, that of resignation. Where pride and presumption rule, there is always rebellion against one's lot in life. Only the humble know how to be resigned."

Leo's face lit up with a new hope. Finally, when he rose to take his leave, Father Lemarie had a parting message, "Leo, I believe that God has a very special work in store for you. In fact, it is a work which you will be better fitted for as a layman."

"A lay apostolate, Father? Incidentally, I remember Mr. Bordier told me several years ago how necessary a lay apostolate had become during the French Revolution. He showed me how the violence of the Commune had proved the need for a zealous, enlightened laity to take an active part in the work of the Church."

"Yes, that is true. Sometimes priests are fettered, and but for the zeal of a lay person the work of the Church could be stifled."

Although Leo's happiness at the prospect of some day doing a great work for the Church was visible to Father Lemarie during their long conversation, once outside, Leo felt quite lonely. Frustrated in the highest hope of his young manhood, with no immediate plan for the future, the stark realization of these facts crowded all optimistic thoughts from his mind. Just how did a young man turned away from a seminary set about finding his place in the world or achieving his lay apostolate for the Church? Leo did not know the answer.

But there was another side of the ledger which Leo realized needed balancing. If it required years and years of assiduous study on the part of seminarians to become acquainted with the deep science of Theology, how could a layman expect to accomplish something for the Church without preparation? Leo was determined to set aside a regular period daily to good reading, and to the study of the Catholic Faith.

11

Leo wondered what his native island of Martinique would be like after five years' absence. When the ship docked and he was met by his mother and the familiar faces of two old slaves who promptly managed his baggage, he felt as if he had never been away.

In the large and elegant house at Lamentin, with vast sugar plantations stretching out as far as the eye could see, Leo was soon in his element; again he was the aristocratic colonial, conscious of his leading position in the community.

Madame Arnaud watched every movement of her son during his first days at Lamentin, for he had written her at length about the priesthood and she expected that at any moment he might tell her about his wish to enter the ecclesiastical state. But he said nothing to her about it now that he was at home, and Madame Arnaud decided to treat the matter with delicate reserve. The problem of a vocation one had necessarily to settle for himself, reflected Madame Arnaud, and Leo was granted a privacy upon which she refused to infringe.

Moreover, these were days filled with happiness for the grand lady at Lamentin, for she had her beloved Leo, her first born, all to herself once more after so long a separation. To have him with her, to hear him speak, to be entertained by his witty repartee, these were joys of which she had been deprived for five years.

"Leo, we are planning a grand reception for you. Friends and relatives are coming to Lamentin to greet the new squire," she told him proudly.

"A coming-out party for your son, is that right, Mother?"
Leo asked teasingly.

"And why not? What have I to do that is more important
now than to lavish my love and attention on the child God
gave me, on my own dearest Leo? You see, my son, I want
you to remember all your life the love of your mother for
you. Though you cannot remember that of your father who
was taken from us so long ago, when you were such a small
child that you could not appreciate him, the wealth you
enjoy he has left you. And when I go, I will leave you mine,
also . . . ."

"Mother, dearest, sweetest Mother, I often wonder about
the Fourth Commandment which says: 'Honor thy father,
and thy mother.' I ask myself how children could help
honoring their parents, if they all had such devoted parents
as I have had."

"Fine compliments, son, very fine, and I'll cherish their
remembrance," she said, and then Leo noticed suddenly the
lines that creased her brow when she smiled. Madame Arnaud seemed to have guessed her son's thoughts, and asked,
"You think I have grown considerably older, don't you?"

"Yes, Mother, I do . . . ." he answered truthfully.

"Not that I am so old, Leo, for I am only forty-two, but
the last five years, filled with anxiety about you and Theobald away in France, ah, they took their toll in strength and
vigor!"

Leo held his mother tenderly in his arms. If all parents
were bound to their children by such ardent affection, certainly there could be no question of so much disorder in
the world. As for himself, he would be grateful for this
warm love as long as he lived.

The ball which Madame Arnaud arranged in Leo's honor
was grand and costly. Guests began arriving three days before the scheduled celebration, and they were housed in
the three-story mansion. The keeper's house at the entrance
of the estate was transformed into guest apartments for those
who came from afar; the keeper and his family moved to
one of the slave cottages on the plantation.

Leo was not immune to the pleasure of refined hospitality

and social intercourse which the grand ball afforded. But to the scheming dames who brought their marriageable daughters to Lamentin to display them before the eligible bachelor he was a real disappointment. Leo had a smile for everyone, and he reaped a visible joy from every guest's company. Moreover, when the dancing went its rounds, Leo missed not one single turn. And though every girl at Lamentin had her turn with the handsome and wealthy Leo Dupont, no particular mademoiselle could boast of having had two dances with him.

In the fall, Leo was offered a position as royal councilor at court. He was happy to take his place in the more serious affairs of the community and devoted his time conscientiously to the duties which his new position imposed on him. Besides being royal councilor, Leo also looked after the plantation. He acquainted himself with all that went on, and if the hired help or the slaves thought at the beginning that the new master was too young to shoulder so much responsibility they soon learned that he lacked none of the exactitude that comes with more mature years.

When Christmas arrived, Leo found himself with a number of invitations to various house parties. Among them, one from Trois-Ilets particularly awakened his interest.

"Mother, I've a load of invitations for the Christmas holidays," he informed her.

"I'm happy you have because I want to see you enjoy yourself at Christmas. You've worked assiduously at court as well as here on the plantation," she added.

"I was just thinking I'd like to accept the invitation to Trois-Ilets," Leo said, hesitatingly.

"Oh, by all means. You can have such a lovely time with Caroline."

"Yes, I feel I know her better than the others because of the summer vacations she used to spend with us at Uncle's place at Chissay."

"That's right, Leo. You both went off to France to be educated there, and so you have a great deal in common. You will find her parents very congenial, too," added Madame Arnaud, happy that Leo accepted the Audiffredi invitation in preference to others.

At Trois-Islets, Leo found himself completely at home that Christmas. His stay of three days was filled with indoor amusements. Quite unconsciously Leo found himself telling Caroline all about his studies in Paris, about meeting Mr. Bordier, about Clement, and on the evening before his departure, much to his own surprise, about things he never mentioned to any one else. He told Caroline about St. Sulpice and the disappointment he suffered when he learned he could not be a priest.

"I had no idea, Leo," said Caroline sympathetically. "It must have been very hard for you."

"Well, it is all over now, Caroline. I am entirely resigned never to be a priest. But here I am, worrying you with my problems. Believe me, I wouldn't think of telling them to anyone else . . . ."

"Perhaps I can help a little."

"You help a great deal, Caroline," answered Leo warmly, and then abruptly turned away.

After the joyous Christmas holidays, Leo came back to Lamentin to take up the routine of his professional work and to supervise the plantation until the heat of the summer came round once more; then, taking a needed vacation, Leo went swimming and riding, his two favorite sports.

It was fall again. Madame Arnaud announced to her son that she was preparing to open the social season with a formal ball. She asked Leo to supply the names of particular friends they should invite.

"Just so long as you invite Caroline, Mother," he said without a moment's hesitation. "As for the others, well, I like to dance with them but they never have anything worthwhile to contribute in the way of serious conversation."

"I didn't think you cared for serious conversation at balls, Leo."

"Maybe, Mother, you don't know me as well as I thought you did."

"Sometimes, Leo, I wonder if I know you at all. You've now been home more than a year. Another young man in your position would think of, well, of getting married, but you shy away from things . . . ."

"I'm not a bore, am I, Mother?"

"No, you're very congenial, Leo. But you're somewhat of a puzzle. Nobody knows what goes on in your mind. Sometimes when I see you continue to seek out the parish priest every Saturday evening, to go to confession, I wonder if, maybe, you are still thinking of becoming a priest."

Leo suddenly looked away. Madame Arnaud was sorry she spoke.

"Leo, you know I love you more than anyone else in the world. Your happiness is all I think about. Of course, I had planned on your taking over Lamentin as your own when I'm gone. Now I say to myself, if you become a priest you would probably have to accept some obscure parish, whereas I wanted you to have everything fine. Oh, Leo, I don't know how to explain it . . . ."

"Well, Mother, although I know you would not stand in the way of my becoming a priest, if the matter really came to a final test, because you are too good to stand between God and His call, yet let me tell you, you need not ever fear that I'll be off to fill the office of an obscure pastor."

Madame Arnaud looked up at her son seriously, and Leo went on, "Do you see this stub of a finger? It is the sign that I cannot aspire to the priesthood but must seek in some lower station of life a way to fulfill God's designs."

An inward resentment, a wounded mother's pride at the mere suggestion that her son could be unfit for anything he desired, filled Madame Arnaud's heart and she exclaimed, "But, Leo, that small, insignificant defect would not, could not possibly stand in the way of your becoming a priest, that is, if you really wanted to be a priest!"

"It could, Mother. It did, in fact!"

"Oh, Leo, I never realized it all meant so much to you," Madame Arnaud wept. "But I am so relieved that you told me. I want to share some of your disappointment," she added. Then later that evening, seeking him out, she whispered, "Leo, believe your mother, who is much older than you, that time—time heals many a deep wound. I so want you to be happy."

In the days that followed, Madame Arnaud forgot somewhat her anxiety over Leo's problem, as she busied herself with the redecoration of the grand ball room of Lamentin.

When the evening scheduled for the entertainment arrived, about an hour before the guests were expected, Leo's mother was summoned to the parlor. It was Mr. and Madame Chevron.

"You will excuse us, Madame Arnaud. We are not in evening attire, and have come with personal regrets to say that we will not be able to attend this evening . . . ." said Mr. Chevron.

His wife hastened with a further explanation, "Our daughter's husband, who you know was a French officer, has been killed. A delay in communications brought us the message only today, though the tragedy occurred a week ago."

"How sad!" came sympathetically from Madame Arnaud.

"We feel we should not delay the baptism of the child who was born to our daughter last week. As grandparents, we deem it our duty to proceed immediately to get the child baptized. We are, therefore, on our way to invite Mr. Boudin to act as sponsor . . . ."

"Mr. Boudin, a sponsor at baptism?" asked Madame Arnaud, and then in an effort to conceal her surprise she added, "But, please, do wait here a moment. Let me have Elise serve you a cup of hot tea."

While the beverage was being served, Madame Arnaud went in hurried search of her son. "Leo, the Chevrons are here. You remember they recently celebrated the wedding of their daughter, Anette, to a French officer? Well, they have just received word that their son-in-law has been killed in France. And what do you suppose they are doing? They tell me that as grandparents they feel it their duty to attend to the baptism of their grandchild, who was born to their daughter last week. They are now on their way to ask Mr. Boudin to stand as sponsor at the baptism."

"Mr. Boudin, sponsor at baptism?" asked Leo, amazed.

"Yes, that's the choice the grandparents are making. I don't know what to think of it, do you?"

"All I can say is that the choice of a man like Mr. Boudin defeats the very purpose the Church had in mind when she prescribed sponsors at baptism."

"I know. It's not right. That's why I came up here to tell you about it. I believe I know the reason they are selecting Boudin."

"What do you think is the reason, Mother?"

"His money! Mr. Boudin is very rich. On the other hand, the Chevrons, who still boast of a fine family name, have lost most of their possessions. In fact, I think they are practically destitute and in their condition have struck on the idea of Mr. Boudin as sponsor to their grandchild."

"Yes, you're right. It can be nothing else. Surely, the Chevrons as well as all the people in this part of Martinique know that Mr. Boudin does not go to Church and that he openly ridicules religion." Leo thought for a while and then added, "But to uphold family finances, the Chevrons are now on their way to ask Mr. Boudin to be sponsor. May God help the child who will be entrusted to that man's guardianship! Why, he won't so much as send the child to a Catholic school. He'll probably have her brought up as a freethinker. I know Boudin, Mother, for we've had it out a hundred times since I got back to Martinique. He'll jump at this chance to be sponsor only the more to ridicule our Christian customs. Then, with all the money he has, he will provide his godchild with everything, including a planned atheistic education."

"What are French Catholic families coming to?" deplored Madame Arnaud. "You never know what to expect next."

"Mother, I think I have a solution."

"You have?"

"Yes. Tell me, do you see any reason why *I* couldn't be the sponsor on this occasion? Go downstairs now and suggest to the Chevrons, tactfully, of course, that you think I would be happy to be the godfather of their grandchild—that is, if they asked me. . . . In that case, I could assume charge and send the girl to a convent to be educated. Here is a question

of the salvation of a soul. If it is only money that matters to
the Chevrons, then I can provide that as well, and much
better than Mr. Boudin."

Madame Arnaud could find no reason to object to Leo's
plan. Promptly she went downstairs and made the offer to
the Chevrons, who, happy and amazed, rose to their feet.
"Your son, Leo Dupont, sponsor to our little orphaned
grandchild?" asked Mrs. Chevron.

"Yes, I'm sure it could be arranged . . . ." replied Madame
Arnaud, trying to sound casual.

"Oh, Madame, if it could be arranged it would be most
satisfactory, most satisfactory." It was Mr. Chevron's turn to
express their delight.

"Elise, go upstairs and tell Mr. Dupont that Mr. and
Madame Chevron are here and wish to speak with him,"
said the lady of the house, addressing her maid.

A few moments later, Leo, already dressed for the ball,
came downstairs in his formal attire, elegant in every gesture.

After a few words of customary greetings, Mr. Chevron
spoke out, "Mr. Dupont, we would indeed be much honored
if you would be sponsor to our grandchild, whose father has
just been reported killed in France . . . ."

"And why not? On my part, I will feel highly privileged
to be the godfather of your grandchild. If you will be kind
enough to tell me where and when the baptism is to take
place, I shall arrange to see that every detail is taken care of."

True to his word, Leo not only made a settlement of a
monthly allowance for the rearing of this orphaned child,
but he saw to it that the Negro woman hired to be the infant's nurse was a responsible Catholic. Once every three
months, Leo would take a day off and ride out to visit his
godchild. Satisfied that she was well taken care of and in
good surroundings, he felt compensated for his efforts.

ANOTHER two years sped by quickly enough and Leo, now
with three years' experience at the bar, was everywhere es-

teemed and praised. Then one Saturday afternoon in June, the Audiffredis with their daughter Caroline stopped at Lamentin.

"We are on our way to the Lakes for a three-week vacation and stopped here for a visit with you," said Mr. Audiffredi, as he helped his wife and daughter from the carriage.

"We are very glad to have you," said Madame Arnaud, and then turning to Caroline she added, "And what a delightful surprise it will be for Leo to see you, Caroline."

Plans were made for them to stay overnight.

"Tomorrow being Sunday, you can attend Mass with us and then after breakfast, drive off to your vacation," suggested Leo, glad to have their company.

Leo realized by now that he grew more fond of Caroline each time he saw her. Just how she felt about him, he could never quite tell for Caroline was always quiet and reserved. But by the time Mass was over that Sunday morning, Leo was to have his chance at learning how he stood with Caroline.

They had gone to Mass together as planned, and hardly were Leo and Caroline seated in their pew, when across the aisle to Leo's left, a young Negress dressed in loud finery, with large plumes in her hat, and enormous earbobs dangling noisily from her ears, was shifting about coquettishly in an effort to attract the attention of her neighbors. A small door separated Leo's pew from the side aisle, but he could not help noticing the noisy distraction. When the priest came out of the sacristy to begin Mass, Leo flashed the girl a threatening look, but this had no effect on her. Even Caroline, whose diffidence scarcely allowed her to notice others, was aware of the distraction, and she seemed mortified and embarrassed.

Finally, when the congregation rose at the preface of the Mass, Leo decided to take advantage of his standing position and, reaching out across the aisle, he gave the girl a box on the ear. She came to her senses at once and kept quiet for the remainder of the Mass. Her immediate neighbors, being spared further annoyance, pulled out their prayer beads and all was quiet.

When Madame Arnaud's guests were assembled at her breakfast table later that morning, the conversation naturally turned to the incident at Mass.

"I noticed that my son does not always have recourse to the due processes of law before administering punishment. This morning, for example, I noticed him take the law right into his own hands," Madame Arnaud said, sending Leo a teasing glance.

"But, Mother, don't you honestly think it was up to me to stop that woman's silly nonsense? She was distracting everyone in church," vehemently protested Leo.

"What do you think, Caroline?" asked Madame Arnaud, pointedly addressing the young lady across the table. Moments seemed to pass into interminable ages as Leo waited to hear Caroline's verdict.

"I think Leo did well. The remedy he administered proved very effective. He restored order and put an end to distraction!" Caroline had actually spoken the words. She had taken Leo's side, and unblushingly. She sounded like one who had for a long time been deeply convinced that to be on Leo's side was to be on the right side.

"What are you all trying to say?" asked Madame Audiffredi.

"Didn't you notice my indignant son box the ears of a colored girl who was showing off her coquettish finery in church this morning?" asked Madame Arnaud.

"No, I did not," admitted Madame Audiffredi.

"Neither did I," added Mr. Audiffredi.

"Well then after all, I believe you were less noticed than I thought you were, Leo. But, still I maintain, Martinique never had a young bachelor like you," she said smiling self-contentedly.

Just then Elise entered to serve the chilled fruit juice.

"And Elise, what about that? Did you see your master box anybody's ears in church this morning?" asked Madame Arnaud.

"Oh yes, Ma'am, I saw it, I did. We all sawed it, that is all us colored girls and colored men sawed it," she answered promptly, boastful of having been present at the scene of action, and not having missed it.

"Leave it to you Negroes not to miss anything exciting," said Madame Arnaud in her domestic tone. "And who was the girl, Elise, do you know her?" she asked.

"It was Barbara, Ma'am, it was Barbara. Yes, we knows her!"

"To whom does she belong?" further queried Madame.

"She's new, Ma'am, she's real new. She belongs to the Boudin plantation. Nobody on our place likes her, Ma'am, she's a trouble-maker that Barbara is. None us likes her . . . ." Elise gossiped.

"I see, you really are well acquainted, aren't you?"

"Oh, yes, Ma'am, we all knows her," assured Elise.

"And from what I am inclined to gather, I don't suppose any of you are too sorry to see Barbara reprimanded by your master, am I right?"

Elise broke out in short, staccato laughs. Sorry for Barbara? Indeed not! Neither she nor any of the outside Negroes, nor even Alfred the house servant, nor his gentle cousin, Adele, the pet of the place whose gracious manners and deep piety distinguished her from everyone, none of them were sorry for Barbara.

A half-hour later, the Audiffredis were leaving Lamentin to drive to the lake resort. At the carriage Leo managed to ask Caroline a question. "Tell me, Caroline, do you think that, well, that perhaps I am too strict, I mean, maybe you think I'm sort of an old-fashioned fogey because I slapped that misbehaved damsel in church this morning?"

"No, Leo, I don't think so at all. You could never hurt anyone. Reprove the erring who come under your notice, yes, that you'll do, but you could never hurt anyone. You're too kind!"

The horses gave a sudden jerk and the carriage was off, and with it, patient, demure Caroline. Only her reassuring voice seemed to linger behind at Lamentin: "No, Leo, you couldn't hurt anyone. You're too kind . . . ."

Twice that morning Caroline had definitely taken Leo's part against the world, and Leo began to reflect that he was not alone, even if Caroline went off in the carriage. She was on his side!

12

DURING THE weeks that followed, Leo's visits to the parish priest were more frequent and more prolonged. He evidently had something serious on his mind again, thought Madame Arnaud. But the seal of confession kept Leo's problems shrouded, and nobody but the priest knew what Leo was thinking about, what problems he carried to the dim corner of the church where confessions were heard.

Had Madame Arnaud the slightest inkling of what was transpiring, she would have been happy, for Leo was wrestling with the problem of deciding his state of life. Perhaps it would be best for him to settle down and to marry. At times when such thoughts crossed his mind, Leo perceived that Caroline Audiffredi at once came to his thoughts.

"My mother tells me that a single man in the world seems lonely, out of place. Perhaps, occasionally, a bachelor manages a useful and happy life in the world, she says, but not a man in my position, who is looked up to, consulted, and always held up to everyone's notice," Leo told the priest one day.

The priest approved the wisdom of the mother's words. Leo was twenty-seven now, would be twenty-eight in January, only a month away. Marriage to Caroline Audiffredi seemed to promise a lifetime of happiness and security.

Leo's visits to Trois-Ilets now became more frequent, more serious, and much happier. As the months slipped by, Leo found himself admiring Caroline's quiet simplicity more and more. As for Leo's mother, she was never more joyous than when, returning from a trip to Trois-Ilets, Leo had pleasant news to exchange about Caroline. She was everything that stood for goodness as far as Leo was concerned and he told his mother as much.

"Leo, I am overjoyed at last to hear you speak seriously of Caroline!" said Madame Arnaud.

"Do you give me your consent, then, to ask for Caroline's hand, Mother?" Leo asked seriously.

"You have my full consent, son, and you have my blessing too. Caroline is just the girl for you. I've waited and prayed for this day so long, Leo. I just didn't like to see you always alone!" Tears welled in her eyes. She would see Leo settled at last. As for her son's choice of a partner, there could be no finer girl than Caroline Audiffredi in all of Martinique.

Caroline's parents were duly informed by Leo of his intention to seek their daughter in marriage, and they gave their consent happily. Caroline accepted Leo's proposal. She was twenty-two years of age; Leo was twenty-seven.

Madame Arnaud's joy was unbounded. "Oh, Caroline, if only Leo's brother, Theobald, could be here for the wedding! Graduation will be in January, which is only a few months . . . ."

"We will wait for Theobald to graduate and return home. Leo must have him as his best man," said Caroline cheerfully.

In February, Theobald was back at home in Martinique. Everyone was now looking forward to a beautiful wedding. Friends and relatives were invited to dinners and parties, alternating at Lamentin and at Trois-Ilets. Affectionate and family-loving Madame Arnaud beamed with joy at all these social affairs, and the days appeared all too short for her to realize to the fullest the deep happiness and satisfaction that now were hers.

Elegant clothes and gifts were being ordered from Paris. Nothing would be spared to make Leo's wedding a never-to-be-forgotten occasion. Then in March, at a resplendent reception at Trois-Ilets, Caroline's parents announced the wedding date. It was to take place in May. Caroline had set her heart on a wedding in May.

"Theobald, you will be your brother's best man at the wedding," beamed Madame Arnaud. "And I will have a daughter of my own—Caroline—in just two more months!"

"Yes, yes, Mother," replied Theobald in a monotone that contrasted strangely with his mother's exhuberance.

"What's the matter, Theobald? Aren't you happy on a day like this? I would expect you to be beaming with joy," she said, looking inquiringly into his face. Her son sighed but said nothing.

"Theobald, is anything wrong?" asked Madame, perturbed.

"Why no, Mother, nothing's wrong! Why do you ask?"

"Why do I *ask*?" said Madame a bit curtly, as if she were hurt.

"Mother, I'm sorry! I guess you must think I'm dreadful . . .." he stammered, "but . . . .."

"But what, Theobald?"

"I've had a headache all evening. I just can't shake it off."

"Oh, that's too bad. I'm sorry, Theobald, if you're not feeling well. I didn't understand and was afraid that maybe something was wrong."

"Nothing's wrong at all. Only I hate to spoil everybody's good time with my complaints . . . .."

"But you can't blame yourself for not feeling well, Son. Come with me. Let me see you to your room. There's no need whatever for you to force yourself to enter into any entertainment if you have a headache and feel badly."

Theobald did not object. He seemed content to leave the music and guests behind, including Leo and Caroline, for whom he had developed a real affection. It was only early evening and undoubtedly all would inquire why Theobald was absent, but just now it mattered little to the younger Dupont son what anyone thought.

Caroline, observant and thoughtful, noticed Madame Arnaud steal upstairs with Theobald on her arm. She knew something had gone amiss, something which somehow was going to affect her and Leo. Her face grew pale, but she looked in Leo's direction, and, noticing him in the center of a group in a high state of merriment, she dismissed her apprehensions.

A little while later, however, Caroline sought out Madame Arnaud. "I saw you go upstairs with Theobald. Is anything wrong?"

"Theobald complained of a headache. I gave him some medicine and made him go to bed. Don't worry, child, he'll be all right, I'm sure," said Madame, cheerfully.

"Well, if you say so, but I think it's time for us to be driving back to Trois-Ilets anyhow. Leo wanted to drive back with us, but since Theobald isn't feeling well, I think Leo had better stay with you," said Caroline solicitously.

"I'm sure it's nothing serious, but it's sweet of you, Caroline, if you want to return home with your parents and leave Leo here with me. You're a thoughtful child."

"Before I go, let me run upstairs to say goodbye to Theobald," suggested Caroline, and Madame Arnaud, noticing the resoluteness on the girl's face, wondered about the reason for the unexpected impulse. Caroline at once took hold of Madame's arm and both were off to Theobald's room.

"Theobald," said Caroline softly, as she came toward his bed, "I'm sorry you have a headache. We're on our way home now and I came up to tell you goodbye."

"That's so nice of you, Caroline," answered Theobald, and then added, "Goodbye," and closed his eyes. Caroline felt inwardly alarmed but she said nothing, however, and, stooping over his bed, she kissed his brow.

"Goodbye, Theobald," she said and quietly walked to the door.

After Caroline and her parents were gone, Leo suggested calling a physician.

"Yes, Leo, we had better call the doctor," agreed Madame Arnaud.

The family physician came promptly, prescribed some medicine, and promised to call the next morning. When he returned about noon on the following day, he appeared alarmed.

"Well, doctor, what *is* the matter with Theobald?" asked Leo.

"It's a malignant fever, Leo, and I'm undecided as to what should be done," he confessed, troubled.

"Is it serious?"

"It might be, Leo, it might be very serious. I don't like the thought of alarming your mother, nor you, but . . . ."

"Doctor, if it's that serious, let us have the truth so that we can attend to Theobald the right way!"

"Well, I suggest we call in a specialist . . . ." said the physician.

"Then let us do it at once without any delays," Leo said, commandingly.

When Madame Arnaud learned that a specialist was being called, she cried out excitedly, "But, but it *can't* be truly serious. Theobald can't be very sick. Why, he's been fine these two months back at home," she argued, but inwardly she knew that often when she studied her son she noticed all too well that he was unusually pale and very thin.

After the consultation between the family physician and the specialist, Leo approached the doctors.

"He is very ill. We cannot tell. Complications may set in, and so, perhaps, it were better for you to call the priest . . . . Should the fever increase, he will become unconscious."

Leo needed no further warning. He must go at once for the priest. If Theobald grew worse, and was unable to receive the sacraments in full consciousness, if he were deprived of going to confession—the very thought was unbearable. Theobald would have a priest! That was all Leo knew. Madame Arnaud might weep, she might faint, she might carry on, but that wouldn't avail Theobald anything for eternity! His younger brother would have his full chance of preparing to meet his God, should he be called to meet Him. If on the other hand Theobald got well, nothing would be lost by his having a priest during his illness.

"Alfred, tell Adele to set up an altar at Theobald's bedside. I am going to fetch a priest . . . ."

"Yes, Mr. Leo, yes," replied the servant, who a few moments later was nervously relaying the master's instructions to Adele. Without bothering Madame, Adele reverently laid out the sick-call articles. On a small table covered with hand-embroidered linen she placed a gold crucifix and two gold candlesticks. There was also a linen towel, some cotton, a silver spoon, and a glass of water.

As she made ready the sick-call altar, Adele noticed that Mr. Theobald seemed to wake from a restive sleep. "Mr.

Theobald, your brother is fetching the priest. Do you want to get yourself prepared? Here is your prayerbook."

Theobald opened the familiar book he usually carried with him to Mass on Sundays. He read the prayers before confession and then closed his eyes to make his examination of conscience. Adele proceeded to light the two wax candles—the priest might arrive at any moment. Just then Madame Arnaud stepped into the sickroom and, seeing the lighted candles and the crucifix on the table, nearly fainted from shock, and would have fallen had not Adele caught her in time and helped her back to her room.

"Madame, we must do as Mr. Leo says. He wants his brother to have a priest. He's gone to fetch him one. It doesn't mean that Mr. Theobald will die just because he has a priest. Extreme Unction often makes very sick people get well. You know all that, Madame, because you once taught it to me."

Madame listened to the words of her mulatto maid as if she were listening to some strange person. Yes, she remembered now she once taught Adele the sacred truths about Extreme Unction, truths she believed with all her heart, but now that her own Theobald was about to receive Extreme Unction, she felt sure that it meant death. However, seeing Adele so composed, she made an effort to be resigned. "If you have anything else to do you can go, Adele. I'll be all right."

Quickly Adele ran downstairs in search of her cousin. "Alfred, come, get a wax taper. You know that when a priest comes with the Lord in the Blessed Sacrament two people carrying lighted candles should go out to meet him on the way."

Obedient to Adele's instructions, Alfred took one of the lighted candles and then they both went out to the gate. The sun had just begun to sink slowly below the horizon when they heard the familiar sound of Leo's approaching carriage. Silently, the group made their way to the sickroom. Theobald nodded a welcome when he saw Father Jerome. Although very weak, he was in full possession of his faculties. Without a word, Leo turned from the door and went directly to his own room where, falling on his knees, he prayed for Theobald as he had never prayed before.

Inside the sickroom, Theobald, with his eyes closed, was making his last confession — calmly, peacefully.

"I will now give you Viaticum, son, and you know what that means . . . ."

"Yes, Father. It may mean Communion for the last time," replied Theobald as calmly as if he were reciting an answer from the catechism.

The priest was edified and amazed. He felt grace filling the room and crowding the bedside of the sick young man like a powerful ray of the sun, dispelling gloom and darkness and transforming the atmosphere with light. Who was this boy, so calm and unafraid in the face of death? Had the priest heard Leo's prayers piercing heaven he would have known that love, the love of one brother for another, was coming to a rescue such as few ever dreamed of.

"Receive the Viaticum of Our Lord Jesus Christ that He may preserve thee from the malignant Enemy and bring thee to life everlasting. Amen."

Theobald received the Sacred Host. A deep peace settled over his thin face. The priest then administered Extreme Unction. When he had completed the last rites of the Church in behalf of Theobald, Leo and Alfred escorted him to the carriage outside. It seemed that Theobald might rally; he breathed more easily and appeared stronger.

But in the morning as the sun rose to awaken the world from sleep, Theobald began to sink. The physician ordered the family to come to his bedside. Theobald was dying. The malignant fever that had caught him in its mortal grasp only three days ago was now stifling out his life. Quietly and peacefully Theobald expired. Leo knew in his heart that all that was possible for him to do for Theobald in those last days, he had done. He felt certain that his brother was safe and happy with God.

13

LEO AND CAROLINE were in no hurry to crowd out the memory of Theobald and the wedding was postponed.

"Seems as like Mr. Leo ain't never goin' to get married no more," the Negroes began speculating.

"Of course, he's gwine to get married. What's more, I happen to know it will be pretty soon now. . . ." Elise was the informer. Since she is always in the know of things, there must be some truth to what she says, they told themselves, and their hearts were lifted up. The Negroes were not made for too much sorrowing. They could work better and be of much more use on the plantation if they had a song on their lips and a jig at their heels. So when in the early fall Leo exchanged his black alpaca for a striped dark gray suit, everybody began to expect the occasion of occasions, the master's wedding at last.

The marriage date was set and invitations were sent out. On May 9, 1827, Leo Dupont and Caroline Audiffredi were to be joined in matrimony at a solemn mass in the Church of Our Lady at Trois-Ilets.

"Where? At Trois-Ilets and not at Lamentin?" the Negroes began to ask among themselves. "Then we ain't even goin' to see the weddin'?" they complained, disappointed.

But Alfred came running to them one day with cheerful news. "We're all goin' to Trois-Ilets for th' weddin'. Every last one of us includin' every pick'ninny on the place . . . ." He was overjoyed and out of breath.

"You mean all us goin' down to Trois-Ilets, Alfred?" they asked in chorus.

"All of us, that is except Mr. Morvant, the white keeper

and his family. They is goin' to watch after th' plantation."

"How kin we all git to Trois-Ilets? And where is we goin' to stay after we gits there?" asked some of the more dubious ones.

"Yeah, where is we going to lodge seventy-three colored folks, all tolled?" came pointedly from an aged and shrunken Negro who, not much good for anything else, kept a strict census of the colored population of Lamentin, no small accomplishment considering his eighty-four years and the fact that he had never held a pencil in his hand.

But Alfred had an answer for all objectors. "Listen to me, now. Mr. Leo is takin' charge of gittin' us to Trois-Ilets, and Miss Caroline's folks is takin' charge of givin' us shelter when we git there. They is puttin' up temp'rary cabins, lots of 'em, enuff fer all of us, right on Miss Caroline's place. And we're all goin' to stay at Trois-Ilets a whole week to celebrate th' weddin' . . . ."

If any of them still entertained some doubt about these bright prospects, they were reassured when two weeks before the wedding, Leo together with his keeper and his Negro man, Alfred, made the rounds of all the cabins on the Lamentin plantation, dealing out yards of dress material, sandals and stockings, bits of ribbon and lace, and other trimmings; for the Negroes were to attend to their wardrobe so that they would be ready for the grand wedding. Horses would be hitched to six wagons and they were all to go to Trois-Ilets for a long holiday. There would be sugar-cured hams and chickens for them to barbecue on open fires. Crates of large, juicy oranges were in readiness for the feast. Elise had been making sugar loaves for the last three weeks, sugar loaves with pecans and Martinique rum sauce — enough for all of them.

At the happy prospect of having a daughter-in-law, Madame Arnaud began to assemble special gifts of linen and china for Caroline. And for the wedding feast itself, she prepared an assortment of her finest hand-made candies, dipped in chocolate and filled with fruits and nuts. For days without end she worked at them as box after box was neatly filled, packed, and then sent off to Trois-Ilets.

All eyes looked at Leo with admiration as he walked proudly down the aisle toward the altar on his wedding day—tall, elegantly groomed, with a white camellia in his lapel. Caroline, in eggshell lace and satin, small and unpretentious, was as reserved as ever. She was to receive the Sacrament of Matrimony and she wanted to receive it with all due reverence. Leo, she knew, would do his part, and she meant to be as worthy of the great sacrament as possible.

"Shall you make your home at Lamentin, or at Trois-Ilets?" the couple were asked again and again.

"At neither place," Leo would say, smilingly. "I have purchased the Hotel des Follets at Saint Pierre, where I have received an appointment to serve as municipal officer. So we will make our home at des Follets."

"But what about Lamentin?"

"I can look after it from a distance. Besides, it is not very far. You see, Caroline likes the Hotel des Follets, and that, of course, settles it!"

The weeks and months that followed were happy ones for Leo and Caroline. Des Follets was a beautiful place, a vast and important estate. It had spacious gardens and a large pond of water as clear as crystal. Leo often went there to swim and perform the aquatic stunts of which he was so fond. The house itself faced the sea and to the rear there stretched a range of hills and cliffs affording a view of incomparable beauty.

A year—two—three and four slipped by happily, and then one Sunday morning, as Leo knelt at the side of his wife at Mass, he was suddenly filled with many reflections. What was he doing for God at des Follets? Here he was living happily with Caroline in the midst of every conceivable family joy and peace, with an abundance of everything good at their reach. But what was he doing for God, he who once wanted so much to achieve something great, he who even thought of setting his heart to become a saint? Leo reached down into his heart and searched it diligently. Suddenly he felt a nudge at his side. It was Caroline.

"Leo, it's communion time," she told him in a whisper.

Leo roused himself quickly and followed his wife to the altar railing.

But even when he was back in his pew, he found his thoughts persisted in analyzing the state of his own soul. He saw himself as nothing more than an ordinary layman. A tinge of melancholy enveloped him at the memory that once a Sulpician told him he thought God had a special work for him to do in the world. Such a possibility seemed very remote now.

14

ON OCTOBER 4, 1832, young Madame Leo Dupont, thinner and frailer than ever, presented her husband with a daughter. They had been married five years. Madame Arnaud was very happy to have a grandchild at last, Leo's own little daughter. She would never be lonely anymore so long as she had a grandchild, she told herself, and Lamentin would be handed down to an heiress. When Caroline had regained her strength and assumed charge of her large house, Madame Arnaud made ready to return to Lamentin.

"Caroline, I am leaving Adele for you," she said.

Caroline looked up, unbelievingly grateful.

"Adele is the most precious slave we have at Lamentin. She is Alfred's cousin, you know, and since Leo brought Alfred here to des Follets Adele seems lonely at Lamentin. I want you to have her. She is twenty-two now and she has confided to me that she will never marry. I am certain you and Leo will find her not only a faithful servant but a reliable friend."

Adele was happy to stay behind at des Follets with her dark-skinned cousin, Alfred, her master and mistress, and the new baby, Mary Caroline Henriette.

Although the child was baptized the day after she was born, the solemn ceremonies of baptism were delayed until June, some eight months later. Such was the general custom on the Catholic island of Martinique. When this great day arrived, friends and relatives from far and near came to rejoice with Leo and Caroline. Leo, always an enthusiastic storyteller, gave himself over completely to his guests, entertaining them with anecdotes that made des Follets ring with laughter.

Suddenly someone missed Caroline, and Leo called out to Adele, "Adele, where is your mistress?"

"I will see. Perhaps she is in the dining room . . . ."

But Caroline was not there. Neither was she in the garden, where a group of guests sat about conversing. After a thorough search of the house, Adele returned to Leo's side and informed him in a whispered voice that she was unable to find Caroline. Turning to his guests, Leo begged to be excused and then addressed Adele, "Adele, take Henriette to the nursery and stay there with her until I return."

Through every room which the Duponts occupied on both floors of des Follets, Leo hurriedly searched for Caroline. But she was nowhere to be found. A peculiar feeling gripped his heart. It was a strange fear, and altogether unfounded, he told himself, but it gripped him nevertheless. Then Leo decided to search the attic. There were two rooms there, only storage rooms and unoccupied. It seemed absurd to go there on a day like this, with a hundred guests in the house, to search for the hostess, for his Caroline!

Flinging open a door, Leo saw his wife seated at a small table, her face buried in her arms, weeping inconsolably.

"Caroline, my dear, what happened? What's wrong, child?" he asked, for it occurred to him that she suddenly looked as fragile as little Henriette, and even more helpless. Leo stroked her dark hair and tried to lift her face. At last he succeeded and, wiping the tear-stained cheeks, he insisted, "Now, tell me everything, Caroline. Are you ill?"

"Yes, Leo, I feel very ill . . . ." she sobbed.

"Too ill even to remain downstairs with me and our guests and our child, on the day of her solemn baptism?" he asked pleadingly.

"No, but too grieved to take any part in the merriment."

"How so, Caroline?" he asked, worried.

"Leo, I shall never live to raise Henriette. I shall never live to enjoy bringing her up!"

"Caroline, what makes you say such a thing? Let me give you a glass of wine; it will make you feel better. And do try to come down to your guests, won't you, please?" he coaxed.

After Caroline had drank the wine, Leo led her downstairs. But the party that had opened so merrily and promised so much joy lost its former gaiety. Leo's spirits were visibly dampened and he could not manage to shake off his concern over Caroline. The guests were not asked to remain longer and the festivity soon broke up.

During the two months that followed, Leo remained at Caroline's side almost constantly. The doctors told him that both Henriette and the mother, although not robust, were well and that there was no cause for anxiety. But Caroline never agreed with this diagnosis. Henriette was quite all right, she felt, although the child too was frail and needed the attention which Adele gave lovingly and unstintingly, but Caroline was sure she herself would never recover.

The summer weather now turned sultry and on the last day of July, Caroline stayed in bed the whole day, refusing all food and drink.

"Let me call the doctor again," pleaded Leo.

"He's been here so many times during these two months, Leo, and he has nothing to offer in the way of a remedy. Don't call him anymore, please," she begged.

Leo slept little during the following night for he noticed that Caroline was very restless and he stayed up with her the greater part of the night. When he looked at Caroline's face in the morning light, he became alarmed.

"Please, Caroline, I must get you the doctor. You don't look at all well to me."

"I don't feel well, Leo," she confessed. "In fact, I've been struggling within myself for the last hour, trying to decide what to do. Now I am sure the time has come for me to tell you to get the priest."

"The priest, Caroline, not the doctor?" Leo asked, as if in a daze.

"The priest, Leo, not the doctor!" emphatically replied Caroline, so emphatically that Leo hardly recognized the reticent girl he had married six years ago.

Leo dispatched both Alfred and Adele for the priest, who, after looking at Caroline, staunchly refused to give her Viaticum, not to mention Extreme Unction. She was allowed to go to confession but that was all. She simply was not sick enough for the last rites of the Church, insisted the priest.

"But I beg you to give me Viaticum and Extreme Unction," pleaded Caroline, while Leo looked on at this tragic scene with white lips, the blood chilled in his veins. This was a nightmare; it was a dream! It could not possibly be real. It could not!

"Mr. Dupont, should Madame grow worse I will be at the Mission at St. Jean Baptiste . . . ." the priest said as he turned to leave the room.

"But, Father," cried Caroline, seeing the priest ready to depart, "you will not have time to return! When you come back I shall be dead . . . ." said Caroline as unemotionally as if she were speaking of the most ordinary thing in the world. The priest looked at Leo, shook his head, and walked out of the room. Perhaps Madame was suffering from a little fever.

Left alone with her husband, Caroline beckoned Leo to come close to her. "Leo, when I am gone, promise me you will send our Henriette to the Ursulines at Tours to be educated there by Mother Lignac. She who trained me will, I know, see to it that Henriette has the best. Promise me, you'll send Henriette to the Ursulines at Tours . . . ."

"I promise you that, Caroline, but . . . ." Leo's words were stilled by his tears. He sobbed like a child.

Two hours later, Caroline's face grew distorted with pain. Leo knelt at her side.

The doctor, too, was there, saying something that cut like a steel blade through Leo's heart. "Mr. Dupont, you had better get the priest to anoint Caroline. And don't send to St. Jean Baptiste. Get one close by. Madame may pass away at any moment."

The curate stationed at the nearby rectory arrived in haste and administered the last rites. Three hours later, a little past midnight, on August 1, 1832, Caroline Dupont passed away, leaving behind a heart-broken husband and a small daughter, aged ten months.

15

ADELE WAS tying Henriette's small bonnet under her chin and coaxing her to practice her best manners. "Your papa is taking us to France and you must be very well behaved."

Henriette was only two-and-a-half years old and whatever it meant to go to France she could not know, but she did sense that something very unusual was happening. Grandmother was with them and her papa was busy with arrangements for weeks on end, while Adele continually spoke of France.

"So, you and Adele is all fixed to go on a long journey 'cross the ocean," the Negroes around des Follets were saying to Alfred, who, dressed for the trip, came to bid them a final farewell.

"Yes, we is all set to go," said Alfred proudly.

"Listen, Alfred, I don' wan' to scare you, but I bet you don' rightfully know what dis heah trip might mean to ya—that is, if what Jeremiah sez is de truth."

"What does Jeremiah say?" asked Alfred.

"Ask 'im yerself. He's here, ask him, go on and ask him . . . ."

"Well, Jeremiah, what is it that you know about this trip?" asked Alfred.

"What I know is plenty, man. I has it on the right authority. Alfred, listen to me. After yo crosses that ocean, and if yo so much as touches the shores of France, yo is a free man, that quick . . . ." Jeremiah snapped his skinny black fingers.

"Whacha mean, a free man?" demanded Alfred, alarmed.

"I don' wan' no trouble, Alfred," said Jeremiah, seeing he

had touched a sore spot. "I don' wan' no trouble. Go, ask Mr. Leo, go ask him. Let him tell ya . . . ."

Alfred turned on his heels in search of his master. What was this talk about getting freed after he reached French soil? Alfred never wanted to be freed from Mr. Leo, nor any of the things he had at Martinique, from the Church and Mass, from Christmas and Easter with Madame Arnaud and Adele, and from all the other wonderful things which made a plain Negro like himself so happy.

"Mr. Leo, is it true a slave becomes freed th' minute he sets foot on th' French soil?" Alfred asked pointedly.

"Yes, Alfred, I meant to tell you and Adele several times. You'll be freed the moment you set foot on French soil!" answered Leo.

"And yo is takin' us on that there French soil, Mr. Leo, and yo is payin' fer our ticket to boot?" he asked naively.

"That I am doing, Alfred," replied Leo, smiling. "Do you have any objections?"

"Yes, I do, Mr. Leo. I just dunno how to say it, but, Mr. Leo, I hopes as long as I lives to belong to you, no matter where, in des Follets, or at Lamentin, or in France . . . ."

"And as long as I live, there'll be a place for you in my house, Alfred," came reassuringly from Leo.

If Alfred's fears were allayed for the moment, he knew he still had the problem of making Adele acquainted with the new developments.

"Adele, did you know we wus goin' to be freed wen we git to France?"

"No! Does that mean Mr. Leo won't have th' care of us any more? But what we ever do in France without Mr. Leo?" she asked and then, not waiting for an answer, she went in search of Madame Arnaud who calmed all her fears.

"Of course, you'll belong to Mr. Leo, and nothing will be changed. Every household has a head, Adele, and Mr. Leo is ours. In some parts of the world, like in Martinique, they call him master, and in other parts they call him a superior or a boss. But the truth is that everywhere some are subjects and some are at the head, giving directions. As for being free, we are all God's children and therefore we are all free.

We need not shrink from being servants or slaves of a good master. The only degrading slavery is slavery to Lucifer, the cause of which is our own sins. Surely you understand all that, don't you, Adele?"

"Yes, I do, only I was afraid that maybe we wouldn't belong to Mr. Leo no more when we got to France," she repeated.

Now that she was reassured, she was at peace again. Adele knew definitely what she wanted in life. For a long time she felt that to be under the same roof with Mr. Leo, to have the privilege of hearing him speak and watching him pray, were privileges any white person could well envy her.

ONCE in France, Leo proceeded directly to Tours, where, without much trouble, he found a comfortable house on Buffon Street, in the Cathedral parish, not far from the Ursuline Convent. They had moved from Martinique to France for the express purpose of carrying out Caroline's wishes that Henriette be brought up by the Ursulines, and Leo was pleased to find that the boarding school was only walking distance from his new home.

The following spring found Leo and his mother, now widowed for a second time, settled comfortably in their new home. Henriette's frail health improved daily under the care of Dr. Bretonneau, one of the most famous physicians in France. Alfred and Adele found life in France was not much different from that in Martinique. After the housework they did together was finished, Alfred would work in the garden while Adele busied herself with cooking and serving the meals.

Leo now began to go out a great deal, to walk through the streets of Tours to become acquainted with his new surroundings. There was no particular duty to hold him indoors. He had a leave of absence from his counselorship in Martinique to which he could return at any time if he chose to do so. But he began to have serious doubts about ever resuming his post at court. Other interests began to claim his attention. Leo found himself once more thinking seriously of becoming a priest. But having consulted his confessor, Father Colombier, and also Mother Lignac, superioress at the Ursuline Convent, he was advised against this course.

Leo now knew he had to resign himself to remain in the world, and as he took his walks he mused, trying to decide on some useful pattern of life at Tours. He was now thirty-seven. He had all the wealth he would ever care for. Both he and his mother received considerable incomes from their plantation in Martinique, and there seemed to be no reason for Leo to pursue his legal profession merely for the sake of gain. He could, he thought, drift into a pattern of routine business and social affairs like so many other people, but he felt that there was more important work to do. He realized he had no one to go to in order to solve his dilemma. Wealthy widowers like himself, seeking a higher life, were not the ordinary run of Tours' citizenry. Leo had to decide in his own soul what sort of goal he wanted to aim for in life.

One day a few weeks later, as Leo walked through the streets of Tours, he fancied a remote plan unfolding itself to him. With startling clarity Leo began to notice that everywhere around him there were ugly traces of the devastating French Revolution. The most recent upheaval, that of 1830, only five years before, was a blow that brought a fearful outburst of violence in the center of Catholicity which was Tours. Where at a street corner a marble statue of the Madonna once stood, now only the pedestal remained with the inscription impiously obliterated. Again, at the end of a street, where a wayside shrine honoring the crucifixion once greeted the passersby, now only the grim fragment of a mutilated form on a cross was visible.

The same was true of churches. Scattered through the town were profaned sanctuaries, with roofs torn off, and debris filling the nave and sanctuary. These buildings, marred almost beyond recognition, were now deserted shambles that pointed a finger of blame at Frenchmen, the children of the eldest daughter of the Church. More and longer walks showed Leo many other churches in ruins and, pausing, he began to ask himself what anyone was doing about it.

Then one day as he walked, Leo noticed a street sign which read "Rue St. Martin" and he recalled at once that Tours was celebrated for the famous basilica of St. Martin erected to the memory of one of the greatest miracle workers in Church history. Why had he never come upon this basilica? In his long walks, he had visited almost every church and convent in Tours—how was it that St. Martin's had escaped him? Leo stopped to look for a church steeple. If St. Martin's Church would be anywhere, it would be on St. Martin Street, he told himself. But although he looked in both directions, he saw only dingy rows of houses. There wasn't even a trace of a chapel, let alone a towering basilica!

Presently, a woman selling vegetables paused to call out her wares. "Turnips, carrots, onions!" she cried monotonously.

Leo, looking down into her basket of garden stock, was unable to suppress a smile. "Would you have a bunch of violets?" he asked. "I could get some for my little daughter."

"No violets! Only turnips, carrots, onions," she went on, unconcerned about the wants of the customer.

Leo was not offended. "Maybe you have an apple?" he asked, trying to be courteous. He wanted to buy something from the poor street vendor.

"No apples! Only turnips, carrots, onions!" she answered curtly. She was accustomed to losing sales because her supplies were limited, and experience taught her to waste no time on prospective customers who always wanted things she did not have.

Leo thrust his hand into his pocket and gave her a coin. Twenty-five cents! With shrewd, slanting eyes she appraised her benefactor and came to the conclusion that he was a stranger, either lost or else searching for some obscure address. A kind of gratitude for the twenty-five cent piece stole into her eyes as she said, "*Merci!* If you are looking for some address, maybe I can help you."

"Maybe you can," answered Leo. "I am looking for the Basilica of St. Martin."

"Hm, ye won't find that, sir," replied the woman. "That's gone, gone forever!"

"You must be mistaken!" cried Leo.

"I ain't mistaken, sir, that I ain't," she assured him.

"But how can the world-famous Basilica of St. Martin be gone?" he asked.

"The revolutionists saw to it bein' gone a good while back, sir. They begunned their black work with tearing down beautiful St. Martin's. Ah, and why shouldn't they? St. Martin's was the most popular pilgrimage in all of France! When they want to do away with religion, what better way do they have than to tear down God's churches, or kill off his priests, or shet 'em up in prisons? Yeah, St. Martin's is gone, it's gone for good!" she wailed.

For a while Leo stood still recalling the life story of this great man. He remembered the picture he had so often seen of St. Martin. On that picture the saint was depicted as a soldier on a horse, dividing his mantle, cutting it with his sword into two pieces, one of which he was handing to a ragged old stranger who stood by shivering in the cold. If the nefarious revolutionists really aspired toward the ideal of charitable sharing with thy neighbor the goods of this world, why, then, did they begin their political reign in Tours by demolishing an ancient monument erected to the memory of a man whose very life was a pattern of what charitable sharing with thy neighbor should be? If the Commune really aimed at a fair and decent sharing of the goods of the world, they could well have chosen St. Martin as their hero and patron!

But in strange contradiction, the Commune chose St. Martin's Church for prompt demolition. Why? There was only one answer: the Commune was anti-God. They disliked the gospel which Martin undertook to preach; for, having become a priest and bishop, Martin evangelized Gaul and brought Christ to men. Martin was no mere humanitarian! When he shared his possessions, he did so in the Name of Him to Whom all created things by right belong. Not merely a glass of water given to a thirsty neighbor, but a glass of water given in the Name of Christ was the norm of St. Martin's philanthropy.

On the other hand, the false presumptions of godless men to share the five continents of the world, not in the Name of the Creator, but in their own names, was anarchy and misrule destined to end in catastrophe. The sad demolition of St. Martin's Basilica, which since the 11th century attested to the memory of a great man whose life was a symbol of charitable sharing, but of which there remained no trace as Leo looked before him, showed a well-advanced stage of systematic destruction by the revolutionists.

Leo could scarcely believe that the Church of St. Martin, which had grown in fame as the centuries marked their dynamic portions of time, attracting pilgrims from all four corners of the earth, was no more.

"Sir, since ye seem to be that interested in this here St. Martin's, I rightfully believe ye might be wantin' to know the place where the church once stood," offered the street vendor.

"Why, yes! Would you be able to tell me?" Leo asked.

"Sir, I've sold vegetables on these streets for twenty-five years! Come, I will show you the square where St. Martin's Church once stood!"

Leo followed the woman a short way.

"This, sir, is Descartes Street," she said, pointing down the avenue. "And over here we have the Rue St. Martin. This is the exact spot where the basilica stood."

Leo instantly uncovered his head. The street vendor looked up amazed. Her experience inclined her to think that no educated, well-dressed man in Tours would ever give external evidence of his piety.

"Would you perhaps know, more or less, the place where St. Martin's tomb was located?" Leo now asked.

"Sure nuff, sir, I know the place of the tomb. What would I be doin' on the streets all of me life, selling me vegetables, if I wouldn't be takin' the notice what wus goin' about on the streets?"

"You mean you can point out the place?" Leo asked.

"It will need more than pointin' with me finger. I'll have

to be after tellin' ye the full story. You see, if you talk to folks that don't know nothing much, they'll git you right off the track. For example, many people will tell ye, and the revolutionists really believe it, that the tomb of St. Martin is underneath that there paved street because that wus what they rightfully intended to do. After they tore down St. Martin's, they figured that unless they done away with every chance of the church ever gettin' itself rebuilt, they didn't do their black job well."

Leo listened, entranced.

"Well, the city engineers had their meetin', hm, the anti-God plotters, so the priest called 'em. They decided to run a new street right through the place where St. Martin's once stood, a highway right over the holy tomb of the great bishop, St. Martin! So after the church was torn down, they begun to run their street jest like what they planned, and you can bet your last copper I come to this place those days and those weeks to watch 'em. You see, I remembered exactly the spot where the tomb was, and I wanted to see fer meself what was goin' to happen. So I walked by here with me basket of vegetables like always, and I watched them careful out of me one eye. Well, when they got right close to the spot I begun to watch 'em out of both me eyes. And what I saw out of both me eyes, sir, I tell you right now. They never ran the street through the holy spot where St. Martin's relics wus buried! Though, I'll grant ye, it's what they planned! I don't know what happened to their fancy instruments, but they missed the place! Do you think that St. Martin, who worked all them thousands of almost unbelievable wunders fer so many hundreds of years, couldn't work hisself one more?"

She paused to note the effect of her story. "Ha, ha, he worked it, all right! That he did! And glory be to the Lord for his powers! Why, those engineers' instruments deviated theirselves, as true as I stand here with me basket of vegetables. Yes, they turned theirselves to the right at the point where the body of St. Martin was buried, and they missed the tomb, they did! And so no wagons ride over St. Martin's grave like what the revolutionists planned. No horses' hoofs beat on the holy tomb of St. Martin! Because, you see, the paved street fer the traffic is there, and, I tell ye, St. Martin's grave is on this side, yes, it's here on this side!" she finished dramatically, pointing an old, shaking finger to a place off the highway.

Leo lay awake a long time after he had gone to bed that night. The ravages of the revolution in France had to be repaired, he told himself. The cruel, brutal machinations of irreligionists to obliterate everything holy from the face of the earth began to have a reaction. That reaction began to take roots in the simple, devout heart of Leo Dupont!

16

By THE time spring came round, Leo was well acquainted with the city which had come to be his home. His days, too, were filled with regular tasks, for the canons at the Cathedral, having made the acquaintance of their new parishioner, asked him to serve as administrator of the Cathedral property.

If, as a lawyer, he was able to contribute his services to advance the material welfare of the parish, he knew that in turn he had a great deal more to gain from the parish priests by association with them. Accordingly, when his business as administrator was finished for the day, Leo would seek out the pastor, Father Colombier, or his assistant, Father Pasquier, to whom he would open his heart as might a young novice. To these priests he went to confession almost every day, admitting his faults and confiding his aspirations. Leo was sufficiently humble to know he needed correction, and, being anxious to pursue a higher life, he willingly placed his conscience in the care of a spiritual director.

In these daily visits with the priests, Leo never allowed himself undue familiarity. Knowing his own station in life to be lower than that of the priests, Leo did not approach them on an equal basis of friend to friend. Instead, he sought them out as guides of whom he asked advice or to whom he confided his plans.

In the fall, when the Society of St. Vincent de Paul, of which he was one of the most active members, decided to hold classes for some one hundred-fifty adult laborers and tradesmen, to teach them the rudiments of reading, writing, and arithmetic, Leo at once offered his services as teacher. Classes were to be held during the four winter months, from November through February.

During the first week of classes, members had to decide upon a plan of grading pupils and of assigning a teacher to each group. Anxious to do that which seemed to him the least desirable, Leo singled out the poorest students and those who seemed least inclined toward learning and offered to teach them the alphabet. After they were sufficiently instructed so that they could spell a little, they were passed on to another teacher for an advanced course in reading and writing.

Three times each week from seven to nine Leo, the refined attorney of Paris, would be at his humble post, teaching illiterate laborers; men who often carried with them a strong breath of onions and garlic or the still more offensive odor of perspiration.

Among the dullest of the enrolled pupils was a young man, a veritable colossus of a youth, with an enormous bulk of a body and a small undeveloped head. Leo patiently tried throughout the school term to teach him the alphabet, but with little success. Yet Leo was not discouraged. When school was let out in the spring, he personally encouraged the giant to return in the fall to resume his course of studies. "You will improve! You will improve!" he encouraged. The big-bodied youth would look up inquiringly at his teacher, doubtful that he would ever succeed in learning the alphabet. But he promised to return in the fall, if not for the sake of education, then to be near his gentle teacher.

But one of the most favorite of Leo's pastimes still continued to be the visiting of churches, particularly those that were deserted or desecrated, where no sanctuary light burned, where only shambles of things once consecrated to God now remained. To him there was no sight so pitiful or so deserving of his reparation as that of a deserted, torn-down church. It was natural that people should begin to notice his frequent visits to these desecrated sanctuaries and that they should comment about it. But Leo would evade their inquiries and smilingly, dubbing himself a "pilgrim," would continue on his way.

However, if the wealthy widower of Buffon Street was noncommittal when he encountered neighbors who were anxious to single him out for compliments, he was not so indifferent when he came upon anything immoral. As he was passing along the street one day, he saw an immodest picture in front of a shop. He stopped, and thrusting his foot through the canvas, demolished it. The owner ran out of his store, complaining about the damage.

"I'll return whatever you paid, but only on condition that you promise you will not display such pictures to public view anymore," said Leo indignantly as he opened his wallet to pay the price demanded by the owner.

It mattered little to Leo that some people in Tours, unaccustomed to such actions, thought that he was sensational. He knew he would go on ignoring human esteem again and again in order to stop scandal.

One day, making his usual rounds of deserted churches, Leo was suddenly caught in a heavy downpour and to avoid a drenching he boarded a streetcar which was just then driving by. No sooner was he seated than he heard the coachman utter a curse. The horse-drawn car continued to rumble on for a few moments longer, and then came to an intersection. Again Leo heard the coachman utter a loud curse.

Without hesitation, Leo reached out and dealt the driver a blow on the ear, whereupon the driver demanded an explanation. "I'm not accustomed to insults. I demand an apology," the coachman said angrily.

"I don't owe you any apology. You're the one who insulted me . . . ." replied Leo.

The driver scratched his head, and asked, "What did I do to *you?*"

"You twice insulted my Father, and any insult to Him is an insult to me," replied Leo.

"But when did I insult your father?"

"When you profaned the name of God by cursing. God is my Father, and yours, too," Leo said calmly.

The driver stopped rubbing the sore spot around his ear. A kind of shame began to cover his weather-beaten face. The shower that came down in pelts a few moments ago now stopped. "Well, I'll get back to me work, and be off, I guess," he stammered.

"I'll climb up with you," suggested Leo, who figured that sitting close to the driver might help the man to watch his tongue.

✦   ✦

IN the months that Leo spent at Tours, he realized many things. This was not the quiet island of Martinique. The French people were undergoing a change, and Leo felt it was not for the better. The Revolution that ushered in an era of anarchy had had serious repercussions on the morality of the common people. Leo was particularly distressed with and angered by the sounds of cursing and blasphemy he heard on all sides.

As for boxing the ears of an occasional offender, Leo realized all too well that this was not a very effective or adequate remedy. There was something he had been wanting to do for some time; he could pray more, he could, like the priests, begin to recite the Divine Office daily. When Leo mentioned his resolution to Father Colombier, the priest approved it heartily. The Divine Office was the great prayer of the Church, he told him, and Leo could do nothing higher than to give himself over to the daily recitation of the Breviary.

17

ANOTHER TWO years passed by, and it was summer again. As usual, Leo was planning to take his family to his uncle's country estate at Chissay. Madame Arnaud, unusually elated over the prospects of a pleasant summer in the country, said, "Leo, I wonder who is more anxious for a holiday at Chissay, you or I?"

"I suppose I am, because you know how I love hunting, Mother, and to go to Chissay means hunting to my heart's content," Leo confessed with childlike gaiety.

"I'm rather surprised. I would think that with all your prayers and works of charity and your pilgrimages to churches, you would have lost your enthusiasm for that sport," she chided him.

"Why do you say that, Mother? Do you think it's wrong for me to be so enthusiastic about a sport?"

"Leo, don't ask me to offer you any counsel. You have passed me on the way a long time ago. I look up to you for example now," Madame Arnaud answered him humbly.

"Now you've changed the subject, Mother. I was asking you if you think it an imperfection for me to enjoy hunting so much."

"Why no, Leo, I do not! But as I have already mentioned, I can't make myself a judge over you. During the past two or three years you've been reciting daily the long Divine Office. You do not allow a day to pass without visiting your confessor. You spend long hours in prayer, besides teaching evening classes and giving your time to the poor. All I do is go to Mass and recite the rosary. The rest of the day I spend amusing myself with Henriette. So how can I compare myself with you?"

Although Madame Arnaud carried her point and refused to commit herself that hunting might be an imperfection in Leo, he knew in his heart that somehow he would give up his favorite sport some day. He did not realize how soon it was to be.

Three days after his arrival at Chissay, Leo experienced a strong illumination. It happened in church, after receiving Holy Communion. As he took his prayerbook to read certain of his favorite prayers, his eyes fell on a small picture of St. Teresa of Avila, the reformer of the Discalced Carmelites.

This small print of the great saint, often considered one of the five greatest women in history, Leo remembered receiving from Mother Mary of the Incarnation, Prioress of the Carmelite Monastery at Tours. He had never attached much importance to the small print itself, but now, as he glanced at it, a strong realization of the importance of living one's whole life for God, and for God alone, gripped him. Intently he continued to look at the picture, pondering every depicted detail. He noted the serious face of the ecstatic, her bare feet, the coarse habit which she wore. Finally, Leo noted that at the feet of the saint there lay two strange objects: one a skull, the other a discipline made of five knotted cords. Leo understood the meaning of the skull, but the significance of the discipline of knotted cords was not altogether clear. Slowly it dawned on him that it was an instrument of penance!

How long Leo remained on his knees absorbed in the deepest realization of giving one's self to God through prayer, good works, and penance, he could never remember, but the impression was so real that as long as he lived he continued to observe with special devotion the anniversary of this day of grace. It happened to be July 22, the feast of St. Mary Magdalen, the great penitent of history. Teresa of Avila with the discipline at her feet understood well the example of penitence left by St. Mary Magdalen since she made it a rule of her Order for nuns as well as monks to scourge their bodies twice weekly.

When Leo rose from the illumination, he asked himself once more, "What am I doing for God?" Answering the query, he shook his head. He was not doing enough, that was sure.

Leo decided then and there to give up hunting. It was the one remaining pleasure in which he delighted, and before giving himself over to the use of the discipline, Leo decided that he could do without the pleasures of this sport.

He left Chissay much sooner than he had at first planned and went to visit his other uncle at Gringueniers in order to visit Dom Gueranger, at the Abbey of Solesmes, only four miles from his uncle's chateau. Since the celebrated scholar of scripture and restorer of the Order of St. Benedict in France was a friend of his uncle's, Leo decided to avail himself of the chance to become acquainted with this unique spiritual genius. Thus it happened that instead of riding the fields of Chissay to enjoy a hunt, Leo sat silent in the presence of the Abbot of Solesmes, drinking in the wisdom of one of the deepest spiritual thinkers of his day.

When Leo returned to Tours, he procured a book on the life of St. Teresa. Having read it, he came away noting one particular passage. It had to do with that phase of asceticism which he now desired to practice, namely, penitence. Leo wrote in his diary the immortal words of Teresa on the point of penance: "I declare that I commenced to comprehend the things pertaining to salvation only after I determined to disregard the demands of my body . . . ."

Leo was close on the trail to sanctity. He had a faculty of hunting down the sources of true spiritual greatness. He culled them from the ancient religious orders, the Carmelites and the Benedictines; he pursued them in the company of fervent priests and religious. When he returned to Tours, to 8 St. Etienne Street, where he now made his residence, having been obliged to move on account of certain municipal improvements in the widening of streets, Leo put into practice the lessons he had learned. In a small closet back of his room he began regularly to whip his flesh with a coarse discipline.

By contrast, when Leo began the practice of inflicting

corporal punishment on himself, he stopped altogether administering physical punishment to others. In the past, being roused to anger, he had slapped a disrespectful person in church. Again, provoked to indignation by those who cursed, as in the case of the coachman, Leo had boxed many ears. But now Leo advanced a step higher. He stopped forever slapping people or boxing their ears. The sight of sin and the sound of profanity and cursing would continue to provoke his indignation, but Leo found a different approach.

To a passenger who sat alongside him in a coach, cursing repeatedly, Leo said in an even voice, "My dear man, I will ask you to do me a favor. Either keep silent or else strike me a blow on the face."

"But why should I strike you?" the passenger asked, amazed.

"Because that would be far less painful to me than to hear you profane the name of God."

At another time, while on his way to a place of pilgrimage several miles from Tours, Leo found himself exposed to the driver's continued curses and profanities. Leo decided to negotiate a bargain. "Let me sit up with you on the driver's seat. It might help you to keep a civil tongue . . . ."

"If ye want to come up here, I've no objecshins. But as for cursin', 'tis a habit with me, nuthin' more, jist a habit," answered the driver casually.

"Do you think it is less a crime, because it is a habit?" Leo asked, taking the seat beside the coachman.

"I wouldn't be knowin', sir, but as I sed, it's jest a habit . . . ."

"Precisely because it has become a habit, it is the worst state possible. Suppose we see a man doing his work so steadily that it becomes a habit with him, do you suppose he loses the merit of his good works on the score that they are now habitual? Do you suppose his employer should refuse to pay his wages because the laboring man has grown so accustomed to work that he likes it?"

The driver snickered.

"Now let us revert to your habit of cursing. It is not only a sin, but a vice!"

The driver looked up at Leo dubiously.

"Now, I'll make you an offer," Leo proposed. "Every time we get by one block without you swearing, I will give you a quarter. We have four miles to go. If you're careful with your tongue, you can be a rich man before we get to our destination."

"If yer serious, as ye seem to be, it's a bargain," concluded the oldster.

There were relapses but at the end of the trip the driver had five dollars in his pocket.

"Now, before I leave you, I want to give you something else, something more important than money," said Leo, searching his pockets.

"What could be more important than money?" asked the driver, and Leo shook his head at the villainy of the man.

"This medal is by far more important than money. I want you to wear it. It is a medal of St. Benedict. It will help you overcome your habit of cursing," Leo explained as he handed the medal to the driver.

"How kin a medal help me git rid of me bad habit?" he asked.

"The medal will help because of the words that are engraved on the medal as also the image of the cross which is upon it."

"Is there writin' on the medal?" the driver asked, inspecting the small disc.

"Yes," answered Leo.

"In that case take it back. It'll do me no good. You see I never larned readin'."

"You don't have to be able to read for the medal to do you good. You see, the writing on this medal is intended for someone else to read . . . ." Leo lowered his voice, as if he were imparting a deep secret.

"Ye mean the writin' concerns somebody else and not me, and this somebody else is goin' to read it?"

"That's right," answered Leo.

"Now, I'd be curious to know jest fer who the writin' on this here medal was meant for."

"It was meant for the Devil!"

"Glory be! Tell me, what does it say?"

"It says, 'Begone, Satan, and get yourself away from here!' "

"Is that what it sed?" exclaimed the driver, but suddenly his face fell. "But, supposin' the Devil is as ignorint as me-self, and he doesn't know how to read?"

"He knows how to read, don't worry!"

"Well, ye see, as people keep callin' him a damned fool, I was wonderin' jest how unedicated he is!"

"If he's called a damned fool, my good man, it's because he is actually damned, that's for certain, and he's a fool because he got to hell through his own fault. But, he's not called a fool because he can't read. Take it from me, he can read all right! That's why I want you to wear this medal. You see, you might forget to order Satan to be on his way, but if the words on the medal give him the message, and he knows how to read, well, I'm pretty sure he'll not be bothering you so much . . . ."

The oldster now became serious. "It's a bargain. If what you say is true and the Divil knows how to read, this here medal ought to plague him like the Divil . . . ." the driver concluded. "And believe me, I'll wear it, fer you see, I've the habit of cursin' as you know by now, but believe me, I ain't got no use for the Divil, no, I ain't got any use fer 'im at all!" he finished, and continuing violently to shake his head, he rode away.

18

"I AM going to write a book," Leo announced unceremoniously to his mother one day, though the thought of publishing had been in his mind for some time. He had watched with growing interest the popularity which periodicals, pamphlets, and leaflets enjoyed at Tours. Whoever had anything to say lost no time to put it on paper and into print. It became evident to anyone who had eyes to see that the enemies of religion were resorting with great vigor to the press as a means of spreading their propaganda. But what distressed Leo particularly were the written attacks on the Blessed Sacrament by Voltaire, who had grown so popular in France.

To undo some of the harm spread by Voltaire's anti-Catholic writings which denied the Real Presence, Leo decided to write a booklet on the Eucharist. He spent many weeks drafting an outline, in which he drew on the proofs generally adduced by theologians, and which required a great deal of research on his part. In addition, he consulted the Fathers of the Church and the Bible, with which he became well acquainted as a result of reciting the long Divine Office daily.

When the booklet was completed, Leo published it anonymously under the title, *Faith Revived and Piety Reanimated Through the Eucharist.* With a few copies under his arm, Leo hurried enthusiastically toward Bancherou Street, to the Carmelite Monastery, to make the cloistered nuns a gift of his first effort at publishing. Although Leo was no stranger to other convents in the city, for he was a generous contributor to all religious institutions there, he felt a particular attraction to the Carmelites, whose life of prayer and solitude he sincerely admired. They, in turn, came to look on him not only as their benefactor, who by his frequent alms made it possible for them to continue their lives of retirement, but as a friend. Being strictly cloistered, the sisters needed someone on whom they could rely when there was something to be attended to in the outside world. And as the years went by, the prioress, Mother Mary of the Incarnation, found herself invariably turning to Leo to settle their business for them.

But she had no inkling when Leo handed her his new publication, on that afternoon in the year 1839, that in the not so distant future she would be calling on him to attend not only to some of their wordly business, but a work as unworldly as anything that had ever happened. The work would have to do with a new postulant whom they had just admitted into the cloister, a young girl of twenty-three whose name, Sister Marie Pierre of the Holy Family,[1] was destined to make history.

Soon after her entrance into the cloister, the prioress, who was also the novice-mistress, realized that her new charge was no ordinary person. Although she came from a family of working people in the city of Rennes, and had only an elementary education, it was apparent that in matters of a mystical nature Sister Marie Pierre was unique. Her interior recollection was almost uninterrupted, and when actually at prayer in the choir or in her cell, she was often granted intellectual visions which theologians generally classify as the highest form of contemplation.

The practical-minded prioress to whom Sister Marie Pierre opened her heart used every means to humble the novice in order to test her. To curb her inclination toward being recollected, the prioress assigned Sister Marie Pierre the distracting duty of attending to the turn, to which bells summoned her the whole day long, and where, unseen, she had to settle through an iron grating the many small matters that came up during a busy day inside the convent.

Before she completed her novitiate, Sister Marie Pierre

---

1 *Soeur Marie de St. Pierre de la Sainte Famille.*

came to the prioress one day with a serious request. "After I had received Holy Communion this morning," she told her superior, "Our Lord deigned to manifest himself to me. Showing me the multitude of souls who were falling into hell, He expressed the desire that I should offer myself entirely to His good pleasure and that I should resign to Him all the merits I might acquire in my new career for the furtherance of His designs."[2]

Realizing that this was no ordinary act of oblation, the prioress refused the novice permission to make it, but counseled her to occupy her mind with the more ordinary way of perfection. Always obedient, Sister Marie Pierre submitted.

When not occupied with any particular duties of the monastery, Sister Marie Pierre, who before her entrance to Carmel was employed as a seamstress in her aunt's shop, made herself useful sewing and mending. She had a fairly good voice, too, which was an advantage to her as a choir sister. But her chief vocation was prayer, which took the form of infused contemplation, and every few days Sister Marie Pierre would return to the prioress to acquaint her with some new grace or a new manifestation from heaven. Confronted with the difficult task of leading such an unusual soul, Mother Mary of the Incarnation ordered Sister Marie Pierre to carefully write down every communication she received in prayer, and to hand this report to her. And this the sister did.[3]

In the meantime, none of the other nuns in the cloister, except the prioress and her secretary, knew of the mystical commerce that went on between Sister Marie Pierre and her Divine Spouse, who continued to immerse her in the ineffable mystery of the Redemption. The effect of this exalted prayer on the mysteries of the life and death of the Saviour was so salutary that Sister Marie Pierre went on from virtue to virtue until she seemed to be one with Our Lord.

---

2 *Life of Sister Marie Pierre*, JANVIER, 1884, p. 70.
3 *Ibid.*, p. 111.

Then a change occured in her mystical life. The Saviour made known to the Carmelite that he wanted something more from her than her own personal sanctification through prayer and penance. The day was August 26, 1843.[4] Sister Marie Pierre had been at Carmel about four years. When she knelt down for the regular prayer in choir at five o'clock in the evening, the Saviour revealed to her the first of a series of communications pertaining to a special mission with which He intended to entrust her. As usual, Sister Marie Pierre set this message down in writing and turned it in to the prioress who, preoccupied with other matters, gave it but slight attention.

However, a few days later when Sister Marie Pierre returned with more written accounts of further communications on the same subject, Mother Mary of the Incarnation realized that she was faced with something that was meant to reach beyond the confines of the cloister. She therefore decided to consult some reliable person outside the convent, and turned to Leo in her difficulty. "Mr. Dupont, in the last few days something quite unusual has taken place in our Carmel. Sister Marie Pierre tells me that our Lord has given her a special assignment. He told her that He was being gravely insulted by the sin of blasphemy and that He wanted reparation."

"Blasphemy!" repeated Leo, thoughtfully. "What exactly did our Lord say?" he asked, interested.

"Let me read you the written account which Sister Marie Pierre gave me, explaining precisely what transpired," the prioress said, reaching for a sheet of paper.

"Yes, Reverend Mother, I am listening," said Leo on the other side of the iron grating.

"Here is what the sister writes: 'Gathering the powers of my soul, Our Lord addressed me in these words: *My name is everywhere blasphemed! Even children blaspheme!* He made me understand that this frightful sin more than any other grievously wounds Him. By blasphemy the sinner

---

4 *Ibid.*, p. 112

curses Him to His Face, attacks Him openly, annuls redemption, and pronounces his own condemnation.' "

The prioress paused for a moment and then asked, "Mr. Dupont, what do you think of this? To us the very word, blasphemy, is frightful!"

"Yes, Mother, but there is no running away from the fact that blasphemy is rife in our midst," replied Leo.

"Of course, you would know better than any of us in the cloister who are shut off from worldly contact. But let me read you the rest of the written account Sister Marie Pierre has given me," the prioress said and then began to read further, " 'to heal the wounds inflicted on the heart of the Saviour by the poisoned arrow of blasphemy, the Master offered me a prayer which He called the Golden Arrow. The words of this short act of praise are as follows: *May the most holy, most sacred, most adorable, most incomprehensible and ineffable name of God be praised, blessed, loved, adored and glorified in heaven and on earth, by all the creatures of God, and by the Sacred Heart of our Lord and Saviour Jesus Christ in the most Holy Sacrament of the Altar. Amen.*'[5] What do you think about this, Mr. Dupont?"

"I think the prayer is a striking act of praise to the Holy Name of God," at once answered Leo who saw in the Golden Arrow a fitting reparation for the outrages of modern free thinkers, anarchists, atheists, and fallen-away Catholics.

"But let me tell you the rest, Mr. Dupont. According to Sister Marie Pierre, our Lord charges her to see to it that news of this revelation be given out to the public and that the 'Golden Arrow' be printed on leaflets and distributed so that people can recite this prayer in reparation for blasphemy,"[6] explained the prioress.

"Well, in a case of that kind," replied Leo, thoughtfully, "where distribution of printed prayers is involved, we shall need the approval of His Excellency, Archbishop Morlot. There may be delays and difficulties . . . ."

"Precisely, and, according to Sister Marie Pierre, our Sav-

---

5 *Ibid.*, p. 114.
6 *Ibid.*, p. 126.

iour already warned her that she would have a great deal to suffer in this work entrusted to her charge. Our Lord explained to her that the more agreeable anything is to God, the more bitter does Satan try to make it, that thereby the soul may be disgusted and give way to discouragement."[7]

Leo listened attentively but said nothing, and the prioress went on, "But our Lord also assured Sister Marie Pierre that although Satan would do everything in his power to annihilate the work, his efforts would be in vain."[8]

"Mother, it seems you kept the most consoling part for the end," Leo said cheerfully, but the prioress pressed on for a conclusion.

"Mr. Dupont, how shall we commence? Would you have some sort of plan?"

"Plan? But, Mother, don't you see that deciding on a plan in this Work has not been left to our individual choice?"

"What do you mean?"

"Simply that our Lord Himself outlined a plan. He designated the press to be the means of establishing the Work! Isn't that right?"

"Yes, Sister said that our Lord told her expressly to have the prayers of reparation printed and distributed!" agreed the prioress.

"But to print and distribute these leaflets, we must first secure the Archbishop's permission," countered Leo.

"Do you think that might be difficult to get?" asked the nun.

"Yes, I think it may be quite difficult," replied Leo.

"Why do you think so?"

"I think it will be difficult because I know that the world loves flattery and dislikes correction. Because Sister Marie Pierre's revelation points a finger of blame at the sins of our modern society, it will require a good deal of fortitude not to shy away from making this message known."

"Yet, we must do it. Mr. Dupont, do you think you could

7 *Ibid.*, p. 117.
8 *Ibid.*, p. 118.

lay the matter before the Archbishop at your convenience?" the prioress asked hesitatingly.

"Well, Mother, I may as well tell you that I'm not accustomed to paying visits to bishops. However, if in the last resort it should devolve on me to make this errand, I will certainly not refuse. But if I may say so, I think the convent's spiritual director ought to be the person to carry this matter to His Excellency."

In the three months that followed nothing was done to further the work of reparation. The matter was kept secret inside and outside the convent. Only the religious superiors and Leo and a few intimate friends of Carmel knew anything about it. However, Sister Marie Pierre in the meantime plunged herself deeply in the new Work.

"Since that communication, my soul is completely changed,"[9] she wrote in her diary. "Our Lord has inspired me to add to the 'Golden Arrow' some other prayers of reparation, and He has condescended to let me know that He accepted this exercise . . . ."

Then, after Communion on the Feast of St. John of the Cross, November 24, Sister Marie Pierre received another revelation concerning the new Work. "As soon as Jesus had entered my soul, He made me hear these words: *Until now, I have shown you only in part the designs of My Heart, but today I will reveal them to you in all their fulness. The earth is covered with crimes, the violation of the First Three Commandments of God has irritated My Father; the Holy Name of God blasphemed, and the Holy Day of the Lord profaned fills up the measure of iniquities; these sins have risen unto the Throne of God and provoked His wrath, which will soon burst forth, if His justice be not appeased; at no time have these crimes reached such a pitch! I desire and most ardently, that there be formed, to honor the Name of My Father, an Association, properly approved and organized. Your superiors are right in not wishing to take any steps concerning this devotion but such as are well based, for, otherwise, My designs would not be fulfilled.*[10] Then I

9 *Ibid.,* p. 117.
10 *Ibid.,* p. 144.

said: 'Ah, if I did but know beyond a doubt that it was Thyself who has spoken to me, it would not be so difficult to lay these things before my superiors.' He answered me: *It is for them and not for you to make this examination. To whom should I address Myself if not to a Carmelite, whose very vocation enjoins upon her the duty of unceasingly glorifying My Name?*"[11]

When Leo learned of this new revelation, he agreed fully that the profanation of Sunday and cursing and blasphemy were crimes that covered the earth. He reflected that blasphemy often assumed a mocking laugh, while at times it pretended to pose as a philosophical attitude, but in whatever form, it was swaying the masses, once by the appearance of sophistication and again by providing the giddy crowd with a sinister chuckle.

Recognizing the deep importance of Sister Marie Pierre's revelations, Leo suggested to the prioress that they be written down with exactness by the mystic herself, and submitted without delay to the ecclesiastical authority of Tours so that impetus might be given to the Work of Reparation in that department from which it should properly stem.

Both the prioress and the convent's confessor, Father Alleron, finally agreed to send the Archbishop a full and exact account of all that had taken place.[12]

Nor did they refrain any longer from giving Sister Marie Pierre their permission to offer herself to God as a special victim. Accordingly, on Christmas Day, Sister Marie Pierre pronounced her act of oblation: "My God do with me and in me what will be pleasing to Thee for the accomplishment of Thy designs."[13]

It seemed the clouds had begun to break, and that a glimmer of light was about to penetrate the gray skies. Sister Marie Pierre, having spoken her words of consecration to God, heard the Saviour's reassuring promise: *My daughter, the prayers of reparation which I desire, shall be printed and distributed . . . .*[14]

---

11 *Ibid.*, p. 145.
12 *Ibid.*, p. 175.
13 *Ibid.*, p. 155.
14 *Ibid.*, p. 157.

19

WHEN ARCHBISHOP MORLOT examined the documents submitted to him by the Carmelite monastery, he was so impressed by them and so convinced of their genuineness that he incorporated the full substance of Sister Marie Pierre's revelations in his Lenten pastoral, an extract of which ran as follows:

"Is labor suspended on Sunday? How many silent workshops do you see? Show me the public places, the streets of the city where wordly affairs are interrupted, or the bustle of trade stopped on this day? Everywhere do noise, agitation and confusion reign as the restless ardor of man devotes himself to business and pleasures as on other days. Here we see rising up on one side costly edifices whose construction God does not bless; there displayed in ornamental profusion are the products of industry. All the speculations of commerce proceed on Sundays as usual, for insatiate avarice knows no cessation. Even in our farming districts, and in our most retired homes, there is a forgetfulness of God, and a profanation of Sunday."[15]

When Leo learned of this pastoral which so clearly pointed out the abuses rampant in France, abuses which formed the basis of Sister Marie Pierre's revelations, he thought it would be only a short time before the Society of Reparation for which the sister had pleaded would be organized by the archbishop, prayers distributed, and the work solidly launched.

But it was not to be so. Father Janvier, a priest of the diocese of Tours at the time, who became an eminent writer

---

15 *Ibid.*, pp. 175-176.

and biographer, analyzing the character of the Archbishop, offered a clue to all the problems of delay, hesitancy, and inactivity that arose in the Work of Reparation.

The following is Father Janvier's observation of the Ordinary of Tours, whom he had known personally for many years: "During an episcopate of fourteen years, the affability of his manners and his extensive charities won for Bishop Morlot at Tours popular and unalterable esteem. But a very great prudence was a dominant feature of his character. Unfortunately, this natural quality increased by his experience of human nature and the critical events through which he had been fated to pass, so that at times it approached such extreme caution as to appear like timidity. His intentions were ever pure, his conscience upright, but instead of acting, he often hesitated and temporized; in such cases he willingly took counsel, but he allowed the influence of his councillors to become so preponderant as to easily divert him from his original purpose, what his own good judgment and sense of duty dictated, and what he would have executed if left to himself. More than once was his administration affected by this, as we shall see in the case of Sister Marie Pierre, and of Mr. Dupont...."[16]

However, if Leo grieved over the Archbishop's hesitancy in matters which seemed to him to demand action, he did so in secret. Even though he was often deeply humiliated by the Archbishop when he attempted to plead with him the cause of Reparation, Leo was always careful to give due submission and reverence to the prelate.

Then one evening, Archbishop Morlot sent for Leo quite unexpectedly and informed him that he had changed his mind, and that he was now ready to allow some of the prayers of reparation to be printed and disseminated, but that they were not to be those revealed to Sister Marie Pierre. Instead they were copied prayers which were already being promulgated by a certain society in Rome.[17]

As months passed by and the Archbishop took no steps

16 *Ibid.*, p. 172.
17 *Ibid.*, p. 177.

to advance the Work, Sister Marie Pierre tried in her own soul to appease Divine Justice for the sins of the age. "It seems to me," she wrote, "that I heard our Lord say, *You cannot comprehend the malice of this sin; were my Justice not restrained by my Mercy, it would instantly crush the guilty. All creatures, even those that are inanimate would avenge my outraged honor, but I have an eternity in which to punish.* After this He made me understand the excellence of the Work of Reparation, how it surpassed various other devotions, how agreeable it was to God, to the Angels and Saints, and how salutary it was to the Church. *Oh, if you did but know the glory a soul acquires in saying only once in the spirit of Reparation for blasphemy,* Mirabile Nomen Dei; *Admirable is the Name of God.*"[18]

But Sister Marie Pierre was also to know the meaning of aridity, when all fervor seemed to leave her. In the face of her great and difficult mission yet to be fulfilled, she became conscious only of her weakness. In this dark night of her soul, God seemed to have placed no limits to the violence of her interior trials. "This Work," she said on June 6, 1844, "is within me as a consuming fire. In all my prayers I beg God to raise apostolic men for this end."[19]

The following summer, June, 1845, Sister Marie Pierre was urged interiorly to ask for a visit with the Archbishop of Tours, to address herself personally to him who had the authority to establish the Work of Reparation. "The Celestial Spouse told me not to fear speaking to the Archbishop for He would accompany me, and would suggest what I must say," she wrote on a slip of paper to the prioress who proceeded to make arrangements for a visit.[20]

When the Archbishop arrived, she kissed his ring and very humbly asked him to deign to establish the Work of Reparation, to which he replied, "My child, I desire with all my heart to establish the Work and to give it the necessary and merited publicity but this is a very difficult undertaking—if you knew as I do the obstacles. We have already much

18 *Ibid.*, pp. 177-178.
19 *Ibid.*, p. 181.
20 *Ibid.*, p. 210.

trouble in inducing our people to follow the ordinary practices of piety, what then would it be were I to propose any
new or additional devotions? But lay our difficulties before
God and pray very much for me; ask for new lights on the
subject and if the Lord enlighten you further, make it known
to me."[21]

Then, as if to dispel any fears the sister might have regarding her revelations, Archbishop Morlot said, "As for your
revelations, my child, they do not bear the stamp of illusion.
On the contrary I recognize thereon the seal of God."[22]

This assurance of the Archbishop was to be to Sister Marie
Pierre a final and irrevocable approval of her way of prayer.
Later when a storm would arise, and when she would be told
to cease working for the Reparation, she would tell others
that she had been assured by the highest authority in the
diocese that her revelations had the seal of God. She was
never to be unsettled on the score of her interior communications, not even by the Archbishop himself who, later waver-
ing, might tend to unsettle her.

But there was yet another benefit reaped from this personal visit of the Archbishop. Relenting somewhat, the prelate allowed the printing of a small booklet which contained certain prayers of reparation together with a Little
Office of the Holy Name of God, composed by Mr. Dupont
with the assistance of certain priests. Not only did Leo contribute liberally to defray the expenses of the publication
but he also made himself the self-styled "peddler of the
pamphlet" which reached a distribution of 25,000 copies.
"Our Lord revealed to me," now wrote Sister Marie Pierre,
"that this new harmony appeased God's anger. However,
Our Lord still desires the establishment of the Association
as he had ordered it."[23]

Moreover, as nothing was said in this booklet about the
Carmelite's revelations, the Saviour complained to her saying
that a mere printing of prayers in praise of the Holy Name
of God would not suffice; that to excite the interest of the

21 *Ibid.*, p. 211.
22 *Ibid.*, p. 211.
23 *Ibid.*, p. 215.

faithful in saying them it was necessary to instruct them somewhat concerning the designs of His Will therein, and that only when this had been done, would souls feast upon the Prayers of the Reparation even as do bees upon flowers.[24]

When Sister Marie Pierre rose from her knees after this interior communication with the Saviour, she felt her own uselessness more than ever. How could she succeed in inducing the Archbishop to lend a helping hand? Suddenly she remembered that the prelate had told her to ask for further lights on the subject, assuring her that he did not object to the Work but that he was not yet ready to give it public stimulus.

Sister Marie Pierre began now to pray for further enlightenment. Then in October of the same year, she was granted an answer to her prayer. An entirely new light was given her in connection with the Work of Reparation![25]

Lifted to sublime heights of union with God, Sister Marie Pierre was now told for the first time that Reparation was to be inseparably tied with the Adoration of the bruised and bloody Countenance of the Saviour. Devotion to the Holy Face was to be the means of atoning for the sins against the first Three Commandments of God.

Having been carried in spirit to the road leading to Calvary, Sister Marie Pierre explained, "There our Lord vividly portrayed before me the pious and charitable act of Veronica, who, with her veil, had wiped His most Holy Face, covered with spittle, dust, sweat and blood. The Saviour made me understand that, at present, the impious by their blasphemies renewed the outrages and indignities offered His Holy Face.[26] The Saviour also made known to me through a celestial illumination that this august and Holy Face offered to our adoration was the ineffable mirror of those Divine perfections comprised and contained in the Holy Name of God.[27] It is impossible for me to express in language this intellectual vision, unless it be by these words of the Apostle St. Paul:

---

24 *Ibid.*, p. 214.
25 *Ibid.*, p. 217.
26 *Ibid.*, p. 218.
27 *Ibid.*, p. 221.

'The Head of Christ is God.' I comprehended that as the Sacred Heart of Jesus was the sensible object offered to our adoration, to represent His boundless love in the Sacrament of the Altar, so in the Work of Reparation, Our Lord's Face is the sensible object offered to the adoration of the Associates in order to atone for the outrages of blasphemers who attack the Divinity of which It is the figure, the mirror and expression. In virtue of this adorable Face presented to the Eternal Father, we can appease His wrath and obtain the conversion of the impious and blasphemers.[28] I also saw that all the blows Holy Church and Religion receive from sectarians were a renewal of the numerous buffets upon our Lord's Holy Face.[29] After showing me this, Our Lord Jesus Christ said to me, *I seek Veronicas to wipe and honor My Divine Face which has few adorers! By My Holy Face you will work wonders.*"[30]

Having given Sister Marie Pierre these new and vivid lights concerning the Work of Reparation, He added, *Now if any will not recognize in this My Work, it is because they close their eyes!*[31]

In the following month, that of November, Sister Marie Pierre wrote explaining additional revelations she had received about Devotion to the Holy Face: *In proportion to your care in repairing the injuries My Face receives from blasphemers, will I take care of yours which has been disfigured by sin; I will restore to it My likeness, and render it as beautiful as when it had just left the Baptismal font.*[32]

Then in the month of March, 1846, Sister Marie Pierre told the prioress that to stimulate the establishment of the Devotion to the Holy Face, which alone could repair for the unspeakable crimes of the age, the Saviour had made several remarkable promises. "Then He promised me," wrote the Sister, "that all who by words, prayers or writings defended His cause in this Work of Reparation for blasphemy, would

---

28 *Ibid.*, pp. 221-222.
29 *Ibid.*, p. 224.
30 *Ibid.*, p. 225.
31 *Ibid.*, p. 226.
32 *Ibid.*, pp. 231-232.

be defended by Him before His Father, and He would give them His Kingdom. It seemed to me that He told me to promise this most confidently especially to His priests. To His spouses who would strive to wipe and honor His Holy Face in atoning for these sins, He promised that at the hour of their death, He will purify the face of their souls by effacing the disfigurements of sin and will restore to them their primitive beauty.[33] It also seemed to me that our Lord said, *Write these promises for on account of the interest they will excite regarding the eternal reward (which interest I do not condemn since I have given My life to merit the Kingdom of Heaven for sinners), they will make more impression on the minds of men than all I have heretofore said to you concerning this Work of the Reparation. You will be guilty of an act of injustice if you do not make known these communications."*[34]

These new lights received by the Carmelite were reported to Archbishop Morlot, but there the matter rested. Sister Marie Pierre wrote her reactions: "Since His Grace was unwilling to come to a decision in favor of the Work of the Reparation I could well see that my only hope lay in prayer through the intercession of Mary, our powerful Advocate. Daily I recited the Rosary to obtain the establishment of the Reparation. Ah, how I suffer at being sole depositary of this weighty secret, which I am obliged to keep within the silence of the cloister. O Holy Virgin, appear to some one in the world and reveal there the afflicting knowledge imparted to me!"[35]

Great indeed was the surprise of the prioress when two months later Leo Dupont came to the monastery with news of an incident about which everyone was commenting. "I have a reliable account of a wonderful apparition of Our Blessed Mother to two small children in the Alpine mountains at LaSalette. To these small children the Blessed Virgin addressed herself, saying, *If my people do not return to God by penance, I shall be forced to let fall the hand of My Son,*

---

33 *Ibid.*, pp. 240-241.
34 *Ibid.*, p. 241.
35 *Ibid.*, pp. 253-254.

because of the utter contempt for God's Commandments, especially the profanation of the Lord's Day and the crime of blasphemy."[36]

Here was the sign! Sister Marie Pierre, who had enlisted the help of Mary to bring about the establishment of the Work of Reparation, promptly received her answer. Through Mary's intercession, two children on a mountainside were now proclaiming the same message which Sister Marie Pierre had been repeating inside the cloister for more than two years! The need of Reparation for the crimes against God!

Then in October, 1846, a particular revelation given to Sister Marie Pierre by her Spouse assumed the nature of a threat: *The instruments which our Lord would use with which to punish the world would not be the elements but the malice of revolutionary men . . . .*[37] When Archbishop Morlot received news of this revelation, he was impressed. "Let all who fear the Lord redouble their zeal and fervor," he wrote in answer to the prioress. "And pray also that I may be enabled to fulfill faithfully my obligations in this respect."

It seemed an opportune time to press forward. The prioress, Leo, and the small group of interested persons decided to work toward having an account of Sister Marie Pierre's communications disseminated under the title, *An Abridgement of Facts Concerning the Establishment of the Work of Reparation for Blasphemy.*

This pamphlet in manuscript form was submitted to the Archbishop, who approved it as follows: "I not only do not disapprove, but I fully endorse this idea; I believe it is advisable, salutary and even urgently necessary to follow the course you propose in giving these inspirations outlet. I am pleased to find in this manuscript all that I could wish to see therein."

In the same letter, the Archbishop gave permission to print a small book of prayers in reparation for blasphemy, includ-

---

36 *Ibid.,* p. 254.
37 *Ibid.,* p. 263.

ing a Litany of the Holy Face composed by Sister Marie Pierre.[38]

However, wishing to conceal the name of Sister Marie Pierre, who was still living, and the convent where the revelations took place, it was agreed at first to issue only fifty copies of the *Abridgement of Facts,* and these not printed but written by hand. Leo at once hastened to make himself a distributor of these pamphlets. The prioress on her part sent several copies to the convents of her Order in France.

At last, no matter what would happen in the future, the nucleus of the revelations made to Sister Marie gathered in booklet form were out in the world and no power could ever recall them. Souls would feed on these beautiful communications, as our Lord had promised that they would! After the booklet was out, Sister Marie Pierre was given a consoling revelation: *Rejoice, my daughter, for there is about to dawn upon earth one of the most beautiful Works under the sun!*[39]

A few weeks later, the storm broke, threatening the whole structure of Devotion to the Holy Face, and the prophetic words of the Saviour *(I shall permit the demon to cross My Work, thereby to test the confidence of My servants)* were fulfilled.

The contents of the small booklet, which treated of the abuses of a godless society, excited the annoyance and disdain of certain individuals in politics. The matter was promptly brought to the attention of the diocesan authorities. The worst possible turn took place. The chancery office at once wrote the prioress, saying that the matter had been carried far beyond the Archbishop's intention. Complete silence was imposed on the Carmelite Monastery and on Leo Dupont. This did not effect anyone within the cloister except the superiors because no one else in the monastery had yet been made aware of the high gifts of prayer to which the girl from Rennes had been raised. In the meantime, Sister Marie Pierre, learning that the Work had been stopped, turned to her monastic duties and her usual prayers. There was nothing else she could do.

---

38 *Ibid.,* p. 277.
39 *Ibid.,* p. 286.

20

ALTHOUGH THE Archbishop of Tours had stopped the Work of the Reparation outside the convent, within the enclosure Sister Marie Pierre now received a final and culminating revelation that was a fitting climax to all that went before. Manifesting Himself to the Carmelite, the Saviour now openly designated one class of men as his worst enemies. They were the Communists! "Then, He told me that the Society known as Communists had made but one outbreak. They await but the favorable moment to rouse and to inflame. *Oh, if you but knew their secret and diabolical machinations,* He added. *Hence, to obtain mercy, ask, then, for the Work of the Reparation from him who has the right to establish it.*"[40]

Answering the Saviour, Sister Marie Pierre said the prioress had already asked this of the Archbishop, to which Our Lord replied: *This is not sufficient! It is you I have chosen as the instrument and it is you who must ask its establishment for Me and in My Name.*[41]

Although shrinking from this new assignment, Sister Marie Pierre went to the prioress and asked her to arrange a visit with His Excellency. Mother Mary of the Incarnation dissuaded her, however, saying that the Archbishop was busy. A few days later, there was another appeal from the Master: *My daughter, I have a great love for obedience. Nevertheless, I desire that the communication I imparted to you be made known to your prime superior.*[42]

Sister Marie Pierre with her usual simplicity then asked

---

40 *Ibid.*, p. 290.
41 *Ibid.*, p. 290.
42 *Ibid.*, p. 291.

her Spouse the following question, "Permit me, my Divine Master, to ask you to explain what you mean by the establishment of the Work which I am commanded to ask of the Archbishop?"

Breathlessly Sister Marie Pierre listened to the answer of the Saviour, who now plainly told her He wanted nothing less than a Formal Brief from Rome to bolster the Work of Reparation to the Holy Face. *If this Work be not built upon a solid rock, the foundation will not be secure; without its own special Brief from Rome, it will languish and die. However, if it is carried out by the formality of a Brief, it will soon be established in all the cities of France.*[43]

Then urging her once more to address herself to the Archbishop, and to ask him to procure a Brief from Rome, the Saviour said: *It was to serve me as an instrument in the Work of Reparation that I created you. Therefore, be consoled; I will not leave you long upon earth after the Work is established and My mercy will recompense all your little labors.*[44]

Seeing no alternative, the prioress proceeded to ask the archdiocesan authorities for a visit. In the meantime, there followed a complete series of revelations foretelling the great world upheaval known as Communism of which the quiet girl from Rennes, now the cloistered nun at Carmel, knew nothing. This was in the year 1847, and Communism was only in its first beginnings. Until Sister Marie Pierre heard the voice of her Spouse explaining the baneful work of this secret society, which plotted in the dark with the intent of perverting the whole world, Sister Marie Pierre could truthfully say she never knew of its existence. "Our Lord has given me a new mission which would terrify me were I anything but a feeble instrument in His powerful hands. Knowing this, however, I am perfectly at peace. He has commanded me to make war on the Communists, telling me that they are the enemies of the Church and of her Christ, and making me understand that most of these wolfish men had been born in the Church, whose bitter open enemies they now are. He

---

43 *Ibid.*, p. 291.
44 *Ibid.*, p. 292.

then added: *I have made known to you that I hold you in My hands as an arrow. I now wish to speed that arrow against my enemies and I give you wherewith to combat them, the weapons of My Passion. The soldier who knowing the origin of the war in which he is enlisted to be the injury offered his King, burns with indignation to avenge it, and intrepidly arms himself for the fray. Think now, my daughter, of the outrages inflicted on Me by this Society of Communists! It is they who have dragged Me from My Tabernacles, profaned My Sanctuaries, and laid hands upon the anointed of the Lord! But their machinations are vain, their designs shall be foiled.*"[45]

Answering this call to arms to battle for the honor of God, Sister Marie Pierre explained, "I have entered the arena to combat the enemies of God. Here are the words of invocation: 'Let God arise, and let His enemies be scattered; let all that hate Him flee from before His Face. Let the thrice Holy Name of God overthrow their designs. Let the Sacred Name of the Living God sow dissension among them. Let the terrible Name of the God of Eternity annihilate all their impiety.' Towards the end, I add: 'I wish not the death of a sinner but that he be converted and live. Father, pardon them, for they know not what they do!' This exercise I perform without any mental effort and with great facility because I simply give myself up to the grace which guides my soul."[46]

In the meantime, elsewhere in France, as Sister Marie Pierre prayed to vindicate the honor of God, her revelations were being discussed in high quarters. A copy of *Abridgement of Facts* had come to the attention of Bishop Parisis, of the Diocese of Langres. So impressed was the prelate with the revelations of the Carmelite mystic that he decided to take steps to establish the Confraternity of Reparation in his own diocese. But before doing this, he wrote to Archbishop Morlot to learn whether the Ordinary of Tours preferred to have the privilege of instituting the Work in his own diocese. The correspondence that ensued showed too clearly that Arch-

---

45 *Ibid.*, pp. 294, 295, 296.
46 *Ibid.*, pp. 296, 297, 298.

bishop Morlot was altogether unwilling to take the initiative in this Work, whereupon Bishop Parisis at once dispatched one of his priests to Rome to ask the Holy Father, Pope Pius IX, to grant a Brief for the erection of a Confraternity of Reparation in the parish Church of St. Dizier, in the Diocese of Langres. The Holy Father willingly granted the requested Brief, and, moreover, he asked to be inscribed as the first member of the newly formed Association, saying, "Reparation is a work destined to save society!"[47]

There was, however, one serious omission in the launched project. Nothing was mentioned in the Ordinance about Devotion to the Holy Face forming the nucleus for Reparation. The authorities contented themselves with a mere representation of the Ecce Homo, and mentioned nothing about the exalted revelations of the Carmelite concerning the cult of the Holy Face.

Although the newly formed Confraternity at Langres was not the full project of Reparation outlined in the revelations of Sister Marie Pierre, it was a definite step forward, and Leo was heartened at hearing the news. Henriette was at home with him for the summer vacation and so he was doubly happy as he sat discussing with his mother and his daughter, now a young lady of fifteen, the latest news about Carmel.

But Leo could not have known that this family joy which he always treasured so highly was soon to turn into tragedy. Before the month was over, a contagious fever had struck in Tours. Was it serious? Nobody knew just yet. Four days later, however, the disease had reached the proportions of a raging epidemic. Schools were ordered closed, and Henriette, with the other boarders at the Ursulines, was sent home until the epidemic should relent.

Although well and cheerful when she arrived at home, Henriette became ill the following morning. She showed definite symptoms of the malignant fever. Leo at once sent a messenger to the Carmelite Monastery asking the sisters to pray for Henriette. They returned word that they all united

---

47 *Ibid.*, p. 311.

to intercede with Heaven in her behalf. When Dr. Bretonnau returned in the evening, he was alarmed. The dreaded symptoms of the fatal malady had spread.

This time, Leo dispatched another messenger to the Carmelites, addressing himself particularly to Sister Marie Pierre. She, who was so close to God, having received from her Spouse so many gifts of prayer, would certainly obtain from the Saviour the grace of a cure for Henriette!

Dr. Bretonnau for his part continued to exert every medical skill to avert disaster. He remained steadily at Henriette's bedside, refusing to go home. He had treated Henriette since she was two-and-a-half years of age, watching her grow, become young and beautiful, and highly intelligent, taking first prize in all her subjects at the academy. And now she was fatally ill.

The next day, Henriette asked for the priest and he was summoned at once. After receiving Holy Viaticum, the dying girl turned to Mother Lignac, the nun in whose charge she had been for more than ten years. "Sister, do you recollect what the priest said during retreat last year? He said that all the gold and jewels of this world are common stones in comparison with the love of Our Lord. Now I see how right he was! All these things are nothing compared to our Lord. He is all, all!"

On the third day, seeing no improvement in Henriette's condition, but rather a steady decline, Leo again appealed to Sister Marie Pierre for prayers. On this occasion, however, she sent back word that although she had prayed earnestly, she could hold out no hope for Henriette's recovery. God seemed to demand this great sacrifice from Leo.

From the moment he received this message, Leo endeavored to submit to the heavy ordeal. Although Dr. Bretonnau continued to exert every skill to save her life, it proved futile. The hour had come to say the prayers for the dying. Leo Dupont himself recited aloud the orations for those in their last agony, while he held his daughter's hand in his, and then, with sublime faith, he said to her, "Depart, Christian soul, depart. Remain no longer on earth where God is offended, depart! Death is life; the world is death. Go, then, my daughter. You are about to see God. Tell Him all we suffer at this moment. But tell Him also that our only desire is to do His will under this trial. When you appear before God, you must present Him the petitions I now give you. As your father, I now ask you to do this. Pray for me, your father, and also for your grandmothers and the members of your family. Pray for all the kind friends who have taken charge of your education. Pray for the excellent doctor who has taken care of you from your infancy, and who has with untiring devotion exhausted his science in this, your last illness, without being able to relieve you. Pray for him when you are before God . . . ."

Dr. Bretonnau, who was known to profess no religion, retired to a corner and wept.

Perfectly conscious, Henriette listened to these petitions which her father told her to present to her Creator when she came face to face with Him. When he finished, she nodded her head as if to assure him that she would comply with each wish.

But Leo had one more question to ask Henriette. "My dearest child, tell me, now that you have received so many graces through the sacraments and all these prayers, are you content, or do you regret leaving anything?"

"I regret leaving you, Papa," she answered with tears gathering in her eyes.

"But, Henriette, if you regret only this, then there is nothing to cry about. For you see, you will not leave me, my daughter. We shall not be separated; God is everywhere. You will be in His presence in Heaven, and you will see Him. I too, although below, shall also be in His presence, and through Him I shall be with you. Two walls separate us at the present moment. Yours is about to fall; mine will fall sooner or later. We shall then be reunited forever in Heaven!"

Henriette passed away quietly. Three days before she had been well and strong, enthusiastic about a week's holiday from school. Now she lay quiet in the sleep of death. Everything dear to Leo was being taken from him.

Leo put away his gray tweeds and every other bit of colorful attire. There was no reason for him to dress elegantly any longer. In the past, his mother might have remonstrated with some points in her favor that he should dress like a young and handsome father for Henriette's sake. But now Henriette was gone! Leo put on a suit of black that he would never again exchange for a color. He would continue to be meticulously clean and well groomed, but he put off forever all the gaiety of colors.

The sorrow in Leo's heart at this last blow made him sever every last tie he might have had for this earth. Hereafter, he would live entirely for God, completely detached from everything. The large dowry he had reserved for Henriette he now turned over to charitable causes, among which were convents, churches, and orphanages. The largest share of his donations he reserved, however, for the Little Sisters of the Poor, and to found a house for poor missionary priests who dedicated themselves to teach peasants in scattered villages. Leo had made a good bargain in his lifetime with his vast wealth. His contributions during the thirteen years he lived at Tours, and the liberality that induced him to give away a large part of his fortune to charity after Henriette's death, still left Leo in good circumstances, but he was no longer the rich man he had been. However, he had no regrets. He wanted to turn his possessions into gold for eternity, not after his death when it would no longer matter to him, since he could not take them with him, but during his lifetime!

21

In January, 1848, the Saviour told Sister Marie Pierre the Church was threatened by a fearful tempest, and He urged her to pray for the Holy Father. In February, grave political disturbances began to be felt in France. King Louis Philippe, who had held the French throne for eighteen years, was overthrown, and went into exile. The following month, Pope Pius IX was forced to leave Rome and to take refuge in Gaeta.

Since the interview with the Archbishop for which Sister Marie Pierre had asked was not yet arranged, she approached the prioress on March 3, saying, "It is the express wish of Our Lord that I speak personally to His Grace, the Archbishop, or else to his Secretary."[48]

The object of the visit was to be the erection by the Archbishop of a Confraternity in Tours, affiliated to that already in the Diocese of Langres, but with the additional feature that Reparation was to be tied inseparably with the interior and exterior Devotion to the Holy Face. The Archbishop did not come, but he did send his Secretary, Father Vincent.[49]

Lest anything be lost of the debate that ensued between the Carmelite nun and the Archbishop's secretary, Sister Marie Pierre, returning from the interview in the parlor, wrote the following report:[50]

THE SECRETARY—Sister, I came in the name of the Archbishop to say to you that he has shown your letters to the

48 *Ibid.*, p. 385.
49 *Ibid.*, p. 387.
50 *Ibid.*, pp. 388, 389, 390.

members of his Council, and they unanimously pronounced against the establishment of the Work you ask. His Grace has most carefully examined this affair, he has prayed for guidance, and it is impossible for him to approve it in his official capacity as there is nothing to attest the validity of your mission.

SISTER MARIE PIERRE—Reverend Sir, I do not pretend to importune the Archbishop anew on this point, or to argue concerning my sentiments relative to the mission which I believe has been imposed on me by our Lord for the salvation of souls. My intention herein has been only to comply with the promptings of conscience. When I had the honor to speak to His Grace of the communications I thought I received from God, he answered me thus, "My child, do not be disturbed lest this be an illusion; it is not so in my opinion. I recognize here the seal of God." Reverend Sir, it is these words which I received as coming from the Holy Spirit that have made me persevere in my mission.

THE SECRETARY—My good Sister, His Grace said this to you at that time not knowing how far the matter would go. Since then he has carefully examined it, he has prayed and he has decided in the negative.

SISTER MARIE PIERRE—This is sufficient for me. I wished only to know His Grace's decision. My conscience urged me to make these advances towards the establishment of the Work of the Reparation; and now having done so, I am perfectly at peace. And I would say to you that my reason for desiring to speak to the Archbishop was to disburden myself of my mission. Therefore, since you are his representative, I now as an act of religion, lay my mission at the feet of the ecclesiastical authority, with whom will rest the responsibility before God.

THE SECRETARY—But, my good Sister, the Association of which you speak is already established!

SISTER MARIE PIERRE—Yes, Reverend Sir, but the Church of Tours should be its depository. I solicited this of the Archbishop but as he did not judge proper to establish it, I submitted; and what proves that it is really in conformity to the

Will of God is the fact that in spite of all this it was established, although I had no part in it.

THE SECRETARY—It has many members here, and has not His Grace approved a small book of prayers belonging to it?

SISTER MARIE PIERRE—Very true, Reverend Sir, but it is necessary that there be a canonically erected Association at Tours. The Work has need of the cooperation and protection of His Grace, the Archbishop. All eyes are fixed upon him because it is in his diocese the Work was conceived.

THE SECRETARY—Sister, I tell you in all confidence that this Work established at Langres is not progressing so favorably; it has excited the comments of the press.

SISTER MARIE PIERRE—Reverend Sir, I am not at all astonished for our Lord has told me that the demon would do his utmost to annihilate the Work. Was it not thus with the Devotion to the Sacred Heart of Jesus, and the institution of the Feast of the Blessed Sacrament? Though the Saviour, it is true, entrusted such missions to worthier souls than I, yet they were persecuted.

THE SECRETARY—Sister, all God's works excite contradiction and persecution, for instance, the Archconfraternity of the Sacred Heart of Mary. This is a beautiful Work including all, for its object is to convert sinners!

SISTER MARIE PIERRE—Reverend Sir, Our Lord was aware of its existence when He asked through me for another Confraternity, and He has made known to me that this first was not sufficient; for to obtain the pardon of one we have offended we must make some reparation, and the Lord has made me understand that is is the transgression of the First Three Commandments especially which have excited His anger. Therefore, Reverend Sir, since both the secular and ecclesiastical arm have been powerless to prevent these disorders, we must at least make reparation to God for them.

THE SECRETARY—Ah, my good Sister, here is the point in question; you say that God exacts this but we are not sure of it. You may be mistaken.

SISTER MARIE PIERRE—Reverend Sir, this supposition is not impossible, yet I am unable to believe that a delusion could have lasted five years as this has, uninfluenced by any one; for my Superiors, in their wisdom, did not encourage me. They even forbade me to think about it and were unwilling to decide the case. The Reverend Father Superior has already referred these things to the judgment of His Grace.

THE SECRETARY—Well, then, my good Sister, be perfectly at peace; you have done your duty in making known these communications to His Grace. Now, I say to you in his name, think no more of all this, banish it entirely from your mind.

SISTER MARIE PIERRE—Reverend Sir, the Archbishop certainly does not forbid me asking of God the fulfillment of His designs?

THE SECRETARY—No, but let it be without requesting the Work.

SISTER MARIE PIERRE—Reverend Sir, I beg you to assure the Archbishop of my obedience to his commands.

The debate ended here. When later Sister Marie Pierre returned to the choir for prayer, Our Lord gave her a consoling message: *You are nigh the goal of your pilgrimage. The end of the combat approaches. You will soon behold My Face in Heaven* . . . .[51]

At the end of that month, March, 1848, Sister Marie Pierre became ill. When the physician examined her, he diagnosed her malady as pulmonary tuberculosis. She was sent to the infirmary. Within three months she was reduced to a veritable skeleton. A high fever and an ulcerated throat which made her mouth and tongue feel as if continually pierced by thorns were a cruel agony but a fitting immolation for one who had offered herself a victim for the accomplishment of God's designs, and which turned out to be those of atoning for blasphemy.

In July, she received the Last Sacraments and was asked if she could have been mistaken about the Work of the Holy Face in reparation for sins against God's Majesty. To this she replied, "No! That I may have been mistaken I have always allowed, but I can positively declare now when on the point of appearing before the Lord that I have never

---

51 *Ibid.*, p. 390.

acted herein by my own spirit. It cost me very much, indeed; but I did nothing except by the Will of God and to accomplish His designs."[52]

"Have you any hope for this Work?" she was asked.

"I have the greatest hope. The designs of the wicked will be baffled. Peace will be restored. How good is God!"[53]

On July 8, 1848, Sister Marie Pierre breathed her last words, *"Sit nomen Domini benedictum!"* May the Name of the Lord be blessed! She died as she had lived, blessing the Name of God, thus atoning for those that cursed His Name to His Face.

Returning home from Sister Marie Pierre's funeral, Leo wondered what would become of the Devotion to the Holy Face now that the Carmelite had died in the odor of sanctity. Surely her life and her Divine revelations would be written and given out to the world. But contrary to all his expectations, Leo learned that the Archbishop of Tours had placed an interdict on the dead Carmelite's writings. All the revelations which she had received in life and which she had written down in her own hand were gathered together, formally sealed by the Archbishop personally, and then locked up in the diocesan archives. Nothing was allowed either to be written or spoken in connection with Sister Marie Pierre's mission.

52 *Ibid.*, p. 394.
53 *Ibid.*, pp. 431, 438.

22

Six months later, in January, 1849, the Holy Father from his exile in Gaeta ordered public prayers to be offered in all the churches of Rome to implore God's mercy on the pontifical states. Revolutionary disorders were shaking not only Catholic France but the eternal city of Rome, itself. The predictions contained in Sister Marie Pierre's revelations, when she said that God would not use the elements but the malice of revolutionary men as a means of punishment, were being fulfilled to the letter.

Complying with the Pope's orders for special public prayers in Rome, a three-day exposition of the True Wood of the Cross and the Relic of Veronica's Veil was held for public veneration at St. Peter's Basilica. And it was here that an unusual prodigy took place, for on the third day of the exposition, a miracle occurred in connection with the Sacred Veil. The Canons appointed to guard the precious relics during exposition, and also some of the faithful who knelt in St. Peter's Basilica, noticed a remarkable change on the Veil of the Holy Face, the impression of which was so faint as to be scarcely visible.

"Through another veil of silk which covers the true Relic of Veronica's Veil, and absolutely prevents the features from being distinguished, the Divine Face appeared distinctly, as if living, and was illumined by a soft light; the features assumed a death-like hue, and the eyes, deep-sunken, wore an expression of great pain. The Canons immediately notified the clergy of the Basilica; the people were called in. Many wept; all were impressed with a reverential awe. An apostolic notary was summoned; a certificate was drawn up attesting the fact. A copy of it was sent to the Holy Father at Gaeta. For many days this prodigy, which lasted three hours, was the sole topic of conversation at Rome. On the evening of the same day, some veils of white silk on which was represented the Holy Face, were applied to the miraculous veil."[54]

Soon afterward, copies of the true Image of the Holy Face were printed, touched to the True Veil, and later sent abroad. Several of these true copies of the Holy Face reached the Prioress of the Benedictines at Arras, who, acquainted with the revelations of Sister Marie Pierre concerning Devotion to the Holy Face, promptly sent some of them to the Carmelite sisters at Tours. The prioress of the Carmelites, Mother Mary of the Incarnation, at once sent two of these pictures of the Holy Face to Leo Dupont.

"Here at last seems to be the first ray of hope that Sister Marie Pierre's mission of spreading Devotion to the Holy Face shall yet become a reality," Leo said to his mother as he showed her the pictures, and explained the origin of the Image.

"It is a very sad picture," said Madame Arnaud, deeply impressed.

"Yes, it is. Looking at the picture we can get a true idea what our sins and malice cost the Divine Redeemer!" Leo replied. "But what I realize most is that it is not the spittle and the bruises that made His agony so fierce. This picture shows the shame and the confusion He endured at being so inhumanly insulted! Here is revealed the Saviour's mental agony. Truly this is a miraculous picture."

But as he spoke the words, Leo could not have guessed that in a few days he would see actual proof of the picture's prodigious worth.

The following day, which was Monday in Holy Week, Leo had the two pictures framed. He gave one to the members of the Society of the Nocturnal Adoration, which he himself had founded two years previously, and the other he hung in his parlor, above a small chest of drawers.[55]

---

54 *The Devotion to the Holy Face at St. Peter's of the Vatican*, PETER JANVIER, 1894, p. 154.
55 *The Life of Leon Papin-Dupont, the Holy Man of Tours*, EDWARD HEALY THOMPSON, 1882, p. 232.

The day was Wednesday in Holy Week, in the year 1851. No sooner had Leo hung the picture of the Holy Face on the wall, than he paused to ask himself, "Can a Christian expose in his house this Image of the Holy Face of the Saviour during the great week of the Passion, without offering it some exterior mark of respect, veneration, and love?"

Then answering his self-asked question, he said, "No. This shall not be! I must light a lamp before this picture of the Holy Face at least during this Holy Week."

Leo procured a crystal lamp into which he poured some oil. He then lit the wick and knelt down to make an act of homage to the Saviour Whose greatest agony was His mental torture, as it was revealed in this picture of His Holy Face.

He later explained his reason for having the lamp to his mother and then added, "Moreover, when visitors come here, or when those who have business with me arrive, they will see the lamp burning and perhaps they shall ask me why I burn the lamp in the daytime, and I will have an opportunity to explain something important."

"What will you tell them?" his mother asked.

"I will tell them that I burn the lamp to teach those who enter here that when the business which brings them is terminated, they must either speak of God or withdraw."

Leo wrote out a card which he placed on his desk where those who came to visit him could readily notice it. On the card were written the following words: "Everyone is free to do as he pleases in his own house; in my house those who come must either retire after concluding their business affairs or else speak of the things of God."

On the morning of Holy Saturday, Leo was seated at his desk, answering some correspondence, when Miss Estelle, an acquaintance, called on him in reference to a business matter.

"Please come in and be seated for a while. I shall be with you in a few moments," he told her and then, noticing that she was rubbing her eyes with a kerchief, he asked her whether anything was wrong with them.

"They pain me fearfully. I can get no relief," she complained. "The wind outdoors made them worse."

"I am sorry your eyes are sore," Leo said sympathetically.

"Suppose you pray before the picture of the Holy Face and ask Our Lord to help you while I finish a short letter I had started. I will return soon."

When Leo joined her a while later, he knelt down beside her and they said prayers together.

"Put some oil from the lamp on your eyes," suggested Leo when they rose from their prayers. "There is an image of Mary in Rome where a lamp burns, the oil of which is often used to cure complicated diseases and all sort of infirmities. The oil has no curative powers. The anointing simply expresses exterior faith, and is an act of piety confounding the materialist who is so blind that he sees the world which God has made but refuses to acknowledge the God Who made it."

Miss Estelle dipped a finger into the oil in the lamp and rubbed it on her eyes. At once she exclaimed in astonishment, "My eyes no longer hurt me. I am well! I feel no pain."[56]

The cure was instantaneous. Miss Estelle's eyes which a moment ago smarted with fiery pain were now well.

Leo decided to continue to burn a light before the picture of the Holy Face day and night.

On Tuesday, following Easter Sunday, a young man of Tours came to Leo Dupont's residence on an errand. He had a sore leg, and limped with pain. Leo suggested that they pray for a cure. Taking some oil from the lamp, Leo anointed the sore limb, and then knelt to say a prayer before the Holy Face. Immediately the young man was cured. He ran out of the room into the garden, overjoyed that he could jump and run with perfect ease.[57]

Several weeks later, Leo went to the Carmelites to acquaint them with the prodigies that had taken place before the Image of the Holy Face. "Reverend Mother," he said, "Sister Marie Pierre's words are coming true. She said wonders would be worked through Devotion to the Holy Face and I can personally assure you that I have seen these wonders take place in my own parlor, right in front of the True Image of the Holy Face."

The prioress listened eagerly as Leo recounted to her that

56 *Ibid.*, p. 234.
57 *Ibid.*, p. 234.

more than twenty persons had been relieved of serious ill-nesses, cured instantly, sometimes at one anointing, some-times after two, three, or more uses of the oil from the lamp.

"Cures through Devotion to the Holy Face?" asked the prioress, impressed.

"Yes, cures through the Holy Face," replied Leo, knowing what the prioress was thinking. "Of course, Sister Marie Pierre wanted Devotion to the Holy Face as a means of rep-aration to God for the unspeakable crimes of Communism, atheism, and blasphemy. But as I see it, since it is already three years since Sister Marie Pierre passed away, and nothing has been done to advance her mission, Our Lord Himself is anxious to prove to us the power of the Devotion to the Holy Face so He is granting us miraculous cures. Maybe in due time, after witnessing these wonderful cures of the body, men will come to understand the deeper meaning behind this Devotion to the Holy Face. It may be that they will come to grasp this before it is too late, before revolutionary men succeed in robbing them of their dignity, before Communists close up their churches, and make them slaves of the State. We have seen enough of this sort of devastation of religion by now, and unless Reparation is done, unless men come before the Face of their Saviour to ask His forgiveness and His help, world revolution will spread, and Communism will enslave us all!"

"May God forbid this, Mr. Dupont. But as you say, maybe the miraculous cures will help to prove the truth of Sister Marie Pierre's revelations of the Holy Face. Maybe the Arch-bishop will be impressed with these wonders, and maybe he will throw open the sealed archives in which our Sister's reve-lations are now hidden, and maybe at last, her life and her mission will become known to the world!"

By the end of the year, so many miraculous cures were obtained by anointing with the oil in the lamp and the reci-tation of the Litany of the Holy Face, composed by Sister Marie Pierre, that Leo was unable to keep an exact count of them. Cancers, interior and exterior ulcers, cataracts, and other maladies were reported cured. By May of the following year, writing an account of the prodigies worked before the

Image of the Holy Face in his drawing room, Leo said, "I have given away more than eight thousand vials of oil. Day by day the crowds increase. Sometimes on Saturdays more than three hundred persons come to my parlor; on other days of the week, not so many. The proof that grace is acting upon souls may be seen from the fact that all understand that the Novena of Prayers and Anointings with the oil conclude with Confession and Communion."[58]

In a familiar note to a friend, Leo wrote, "They have established a sort of pilgrimage in the Rue St. Etienne. The weak things of the world, and base things, and things that are not, hath God chosen. I permit myself the liberty of saying to our Lord, 'Why has Thou chosen the house of the poor pilgrim of the Rue St. Etienne for the performance of such works?' Alas, so many others will say the same with a shrug of the shoulders!"[59]

Leo managed to retain a gentle sense of irony even in the midst of stupendous prodigies.

It was three years now since Leo had begun his Devotion to the Holy Face by hanging in his parlor the Vera Effigies, and henceforth it was to fill his whole life. Taking a photograph of his picture of the Holy Face, he had 25,000 lithograph copies made and distributed at his own expense.

Even more remarkable was his patience and toil in personally preparing the small bottles of oil from his lamp for distribution to those who requested it. Sitting at a small table in a corner of his salon, with many rows of tiny bottles symmetrically arranged before him, he would himself fill the tiny bottles, using a small funnel expressly made for this purpose. Then with meticulous care he would personally fit a small cork into each tiny bottle; he engaged help only to pack and tie the parcels.

"Would you believe it," he said in 1854, only three years since the first miraculous cure, "that approximately 60,000 little bottles of this oil have been given away!"[60]

Requests for oil poured into Leo's home not only from

---

58 *Ibid.*, p. 235.
59 *Ibid.*, pp. 235, 236.
60 *Ibid.*, p. 240.

France, but from distant parts of Europe, and even from America. The postman in Tours often found himself with a stack of letters from various parts of the world addressed simply to "The Holy Man of Tours," and he knew they were meant for Leo Dupont on the Rue St. Etienne.

Many certificates signed by reputed physicians attesting to the miraculous power of the holy oil and the Devotion to the Holy Face came to the home of the man who called himself a "pilgrim." But he was no longer the free person he used to be, who could take trips to visit numerous churches and make his charitable rounds of sanctuaries. He was now nearly sixty years old and confined to his home, almost like a prisoner, because of the continual stream of people who came to St. Etienne Street to seek a cure.

"Do you think I am a physician?" he would sometimes ask. But giving in, he would add, "Come, let us pray before the Holy Face."

If the visitor seeking a cure should be a man, Leo would himself anoint his sore leg, or arm or forehead, as the case might be. If the visitor seeking to be cured should be a woman, however, Leo would order a visiting lady to make the anointings in another room. To give even a sketchy account of the numberless miracles that took place in Leo Dupont's home, and those that were reported to him in duly signed certificates, would require more than one heavy volume. And while Leo was extremely gratified with the spread of the Devotion to the Holy Face, as it received impetus through the many miraculous cures worked through the anointing with the oil that burned before the picture of the Holy Face, yet it was something more than the cure of the sick which Leo desired above all. Reparation for the crimes of Communism, to prevent world revolution and catastrophe, was the prime motive for the Devotion to the Holy Face, and although three years had elapsed since it pleased God to attest the power of this Devotion by granting numberless miracles, the diocesan authorities at Tours, who knew of these prodigies, continued to keep the mission of Sister Marie Pierre shrouded in secrecy.

Then one day, Leo had two visitors, a young priest and a lay companion, who came all the way from Paris.

"Mr. Dupont, we came to pay you a very special visit," said one of the two visitors. It was the layman who spoke.

"Come right in," answered Leo cordially, and then turning to the priest with the usual deference he always entertained for the clergy, he added, "Father, I hope you have had a good journey," but the priest only nodded and said nothing.

The layman began to stammer an explanation. "Mr. Dupont, this is Father Musy. He is unable to speak. He lost his voice four years ago, as a result of a throat infection."

Leo beckoned his visitors to sit down. The layman went on. "We had the privilege of meeting your Archbishop, Cardinal Morlot, who came to Paris to bless the marriage of Father Musy's brother. At the wedding, the Cardinal told us about the many wonderful cures that take place in your house through the veneration of the Holy Face and the anointing with the oil that burns in a lamp before it. The Cardinal suggested that we make a trip to Tours and visit your home in order to seek a cure for Father Musy's infected throat, so that he could regain the use of his speech . . . ."

"You say that Cardinal Morlot sent you here?" asked Leo, hardly able to believe the words. Sister Marie Pierre had been dead five years now, and her writings explaining the revelations she had had concerning the Devotion to the Holy Face continued to be kept sealed in the diocesan archives. As yet nothing was allowed to be written about her mission. But today two visitors had come to St. Etienne Street at the invitation of Cardinal Morlot to seek a miraculous cure through Devotion to the Holy Face, through the very prayers which Sister Marie Pierre had composed! This could mean only one thing to Leo. It meant that the Cardinal was at last convinced of the validity of Sister Marie Pierre's mission. Leo began to hope with all his heart for a complete cure of the priest's throat, and the restoration of his voice, through the efficacy of the Devotion to the Holy Face. This miracle, if granted, might be the turning point that would induce the Cardinal to open the sealed archives and give the world all the details of the exquisite intellectual revelations which

Sister Marie Pierre had received from Heaven during her lifetime at Carmel. Leo now asked his visitors to come to the parlor.

"This is the miraculous image of the Holy Face, a true copy of the Sacred Countenance as it was imprinted on Veronica's Veil when she wiped the Face of Jesus as He went up to Calvary. This is the small lamp which burns day and night, the oil from which has brought cures to numerous afflicted persons. We will now kneel down to recite the Litany of the Holy Face, composed by a very saintly nun, Sister Marie Pierre, and also other prayers, the power of which has been proved so efficacious. Finally, we shall proceed to anoint Father Musy's throat, begging God to restore his voice to him, a cure which you say medical science was unable to effect."

All three men knelt down.

Leo began, "In the name of the Father and of the Son and of the Holy Ghost, Amen. Lord have mercy on us, Christ have mercy on us, Holy Virgin Mary, pray for us."

There was in the tone of Leo's voice a quiet ardor which the two visitors thought they had never heard before. He seemed to speak with God as if He knew Him intimately. He appeared, moreover, as one who had great confidence. But above all, he sounded as one who wanted a great favor and who recognized the infinite distance between himself, the creature, and the One Whom he importuned, the Creator. He was determined to set his foot on a sure foundation, so he first begged the mercy of God, and then the help of the Virgin, Mother of God. Then he was ready to make his petition through the power of the Holy Face: "Oh, adorable Face which was adored with profound respect by Mary and Joseph when they saw Thee for the first time—Oh, Adorable Face" — through all the invocations of the inspired Litany ending with, "Oh, adorable Face which will appear at the end of time, in the clouds with great power and majesty, Oh, adorable Face which will cause sinners to tremble, Oh, adorable Face which will fill the just with joy for all eternity, have mercy on us."

Leo paused for a moment and then resumed praying: "I

salute, adore and love Thee, Oh, adorable Face of Jesus, my Beloved, noble Seal of the Divinity! With all the powers of my soul I apply myself to Thee, most humbly pray Thee to imprint in us all the features of Thy Divine Likeness. Amen."

In a modulated voice, Leo then announced, "Now we will recite the 'Golden Arrow,' which is an act of praise of the Holy Name of God, the aim and purpose of the Devotion to the Holy Face." Then raising his face to the picture of the Holy Face he said, "May the most holy, most sacred, most adorable, most incomprehensible and ineffable Name of God be praised, blessed, loved, adored and glorified in Heaven and on earth, by all the creatures of God, and by the Sacred Heart of our Lord and Saviour Jesus Christ in the Most Holy Sacrament of the Altar. Amen."

Leo now arose from his knees, while the priest and his lay companion looked on with tense emotion. They saw their host dip his finger into the oil lamp in which a small burning wick flickered palely in the daylight.

"We will now anoint your throat, Father Musy," Leo said simply, as he made the unction, praying aloud the efficacious prayer of St. Francis of Assisi: "May the Lord bless thee and keep thee. May the Lord show thee His Face and have mercy on thee. May the Lord turn His countenance towards thee and give thee peace. *Sit Nomen Domini benedictum.*"

The prayers and anointing being finished, Leo turned to address the priest, "Now, Father, repeat after me the words, 'May the Name of the Lord be forever praised.'"

Looking up at Leo and quite without realizing it, Father Musy was saying in a clear, normal voice, "May the Name of the Lord be forever praised."

Father Musy had received his cure! He was granted an instantaneous and permanent restoration of his voice.

✦   ✦

THE next two weeks Leo spent in hopeful anticipation of hearing favorably from Cardinal Morlot. Would the miraculous cure of Father Musy's throat finally incline the Car-

dinal to give his approval to the mission of Sister Marie
Pierre? As he mused on this possibility, Leo was suddenly
surprised by a second visit from Father Musy.

"Mr. Dupont, I brought my mother, also some members
of my family and a few friends from Paris to meet you, and
to return our grateful thanks before the picture of the Holy
Face in your parlor."

Leo opened the doors to admit the large party that followed Father Musy into the room. Gratitude for a favor received was a laudable disposition, and Leo was happy to give
of his time to join the group before the Holy Face to render
thanks. He lived only for God, and here was one more occasion to make an act of worship to Him Whom He loved.
So they all knelt and prayed before the miraculous picture.

As always, showing much deference to the priesthood, Leo
invited Father Musy and his visitors to sit down.

"We've been overjoyed ever since Father Musy received
the extraordinary grace of a miraculous cure in your home,
Mr. Dupont," said the cured priest's mother.

"Yes, we are all very happy," added Father Musy. "And
let me also tell you that when I called on Cardinal Morlot to
acquaint him with the news of my cure, he was moved and
edified beyond limits!"

"Did you say the Cardinal was moved?" asked Leo.

"Oh, yes, indeed! You see, it was Cardinal Morlot who in
the first place advised me to come to your home in search
of a cure through the Holy Face," said the priest with such
evident emotion that Leo looked up astonished.

"And did the Cardinal mention anything about taking
steps to establish the Devotion to the Holy Face?" Leo asked
pointedly. After all, he wanted to know where he stood in
regard to the Cardinal, in the one most important affair of
his life, the great mission of Sister Marie Pierre, and there
was no use in hiding it.

"But, Mr. Dupont, I don't understand what you mean.
You, certainly, have the Devotion to the Holy Face, here in
Tours, right in your home. Is there something else, some-
thing more that the Cardinal should do?" asked Father Musy.

Leo wiped his forehead. He had already said too much.

"Just let the matter rest, Father, just let it rest. But as regards the Devotion to the Holy Face in the city of Tours, let me assure you that what you see of it carried on here in my parlor is only the simple private devotion of a member of the Catholic Church!"

The priest appeared more puzzled than ever. What did Mr. Dupont seem to want from Cardinal Morlot? The prelate appeared very eager and enthusiastic about Devotion to the Holy Face, or else he would never have recommended a visit to St. Etienne Street as he did. Leo could see that he had made an unfavorable impression. He wanted with all his heart to tell this clergyman about the revelations of Sister Marie Pierre that were sealed up in the diocesan archives; he wanted to make this priest a zealous propagator of the new Devotion, but his lips were sealed. Leo suddenly wished that his visitors would go, that they would go back to Paris and leave him in peace. He had to exert strong control to force himself to hear what Madame Musy was now saying to him.

"Mr. Dupont, I want to confess to you that the main object of my visit here was to get some relief from my ailing limbs. I walk with such great difficulty and pain, that I must count every step I take. Do you suppose we could now pray before the Holy Face, and use the holy oil to obtain a cure for me?"

Leo was disheartened. He thought they had come to offer thanks for the priest's miraculous cure, but now he learned what they really wanted was another miracle. Moreover, he had hoped Father Musy's cure would have induced Cardinal Morlot to give his official seal of approval to the Work of the Holy Face, so that they could approach Rome for a Brief. But the miraculous cure had no such effect at all! It only induced the priest's mother to come in search of relief for her ailing body.

Where, oh where was all this leading Leo? For five years he had been dealing with sick and crippled people. For five years he had bent over their ulcers and sores and wounds. He was no physician. He was a lawyer. Not his to repair the ravages of illness in the body but to adjust infringements against law, order, and justice! Suddenly Leo became aware of his distractions. What was he thinking about now? He had given up his practice of law twenty years ago. By a special grace and through close contact with the Carmelite Monastery he had been allowed to know of the infringements against the Divine Justice which revolutionary men were perpetrating, and he had been called to work toward the reparation of those moral crimes against God, through the beautiful and excellent Devotion to the Sacred Countenance of the Saviour.

A partial peace was restored in his soul, and then another temptation took hold of him. Yes, it was to work for God, directly for God, through a lifetime dedicated to prayer and reparation, that he set himself with determined purpose. But, by strange contradiction, he thought he had strayed from his course. Leo hoped every Bishop in the world would introduce Devotion to the Holy Face in his diocese, and that every priest would work toward the establishment of Reparation in his parish. Instead, the Archbishop, who had known him for twelve years, sent him a patient to cure, and a priest brought him a mother with aching limbs to relieve. Communism was on the very doorstep of Christian civilization, threatening to destroy religion by militaristic means. Leo knew the weapon with which to crush it, and yet he was forced to look upon that weapon as it lay fallow. Every family ought to venerate in their homes the Holy Face imprinted on Veronica's Veil and thus stem the most destructive evil that ever appeared on the face of the earth—militant atheism enthroned as a world state. But the very name of the sister to whom the Saviour revealed the Secret Weapon, "Reparation Through Devotion to the Holy Face," was not allowed to be mentioned in connection with this mission!

Had Leo's spiritualness been one iota less genuine than it was, he might have stumbled at this juncture. Turning to his visitors, he might have told them in his impeccable magisterial maner to go to a clinic instead of his private oratory. But Leo, a man of Job's patience, turned now to the stooped and ailing old lady and said, "Yes, Madame, if you have faith and wish to ask Our Lord for a cure, we will all kneel down to pray."

The group went down on their knees before the Image of Christ's Holy Face. Leo then said the prayers. Having finished, he instructed one of the ladies in the party to proceed with the anointing, after which Madame Musy was asked to rise and to try walking. Taking a few steps, she found most of the pain had gone. Although not completely cured, she walked with noticeable improvement. She was an old woman and could not be expected to get around like a young person, but she readily admitted she was much better, as, indeed, proved to be the case. Leo, no stranger to prodigies, having witnessed them in his parlor day after day, was not surprised that God should give Himself in mercy again and again, even, if it seemed at times to contradict His plan to show such mercy.

"Oh, thank you, Mr. Dupont, thank you," the elderly lady repeated.

"Don't thank me. You must thank God. I am but a poor man without any power. But God who gave you being, also gave you a miraculous cure." It was always Leo's answer. He knew no other. There would have been no prodigies in the parlor on St. Etienne Street if the "pilgrim" had not mastered the art of self-abasement.

Enthused about her cure, Madame Musy said, "Before we return to Paris, we will call on Cardinal Morlot and acquaint him with this new favor granted to us. He will be very happy to hear of it!"

Leo seemed heartened. If these people from Paris, friends of the Cardinal, report this second wonder to him, perhaps something will come of it. Always there was hope in Leo's heart. Maybe this miracle would do the work! It was always the same with Leo. Maybe this time, maybe this time! Looking to the future, he always expected a turn for the better.

Then, as it was growing late in the day, Leo rose to make his apologies in order to attend to his routine business. He noticed one of the ladies in Father Musy's party approach him. She was small and very thin, perhaps twenty-five years old. Leo bent down to hear what she was saying, for her voice was very low.

"Mr. Dupont, I also came here to be cured," she said.

The very atmosphere of the room became tense. They all knew the young lady had come with them for the express purpose of seeking a cure, and now that she made known her desire to Leo Dupont, all held their breath to see what he would say and do.

"Young lady, are you ill?" Leo asked her.

"Yes, sir, I am very ill. I have been unable to go to work for two years. You see, Mr. Dupont, I have a terrible cancer with three frightful wounds!"

"Come, we will pray," said Leo tersely, and again the same ritual was repeated. When it was time for the anointing with the oil, Leo as usual called on a lady to make the unction. "Madame Viot, will you take the sick person to the closet and anoint her with the oil from the lamp," Leo asked quietly.

Madame Viot willingly performed the charitable service, and when it was finished, the two ladies came forward.

"I am no better, Mr. Dupont," confessed the cancer patient, disappointed.

"We must pray again," answered Leo, who at once knelt and began addressing another petition before the Sacred Face of Jesus. Then he said, "Miss Viot, now take the sick young lady to the closet again and anoint her with the holy oil."

Miss Viot did so.

"But I am not a bit better," complained the worn-out patient dejectedly as she came back from the second anointing.

"We will pray again," said Leo who knelt for a third time to address his petition to God, the Creator of the universe, and then ordered Madame Viot to make a third unction in the closet; but there was still no improvement. Leo urged a fourth invocation before the Holy Face and a fourth unction; and again a fifth time he dropped on his knees and begged a cure, and then ordered a fifth unction.

Father Musy, a priest accustomed to the spiritual, looked bewildered as he wiped the perspiration from his forehead. What was this extraordinary man of God determined to do? Would he constrain the Divine Majesty? Father Musy began to wonder if it were right for a human to carry a case to these extremes, but at the same time he felt it would be wrong for him to speak out against further prayers and anointings. He remembered all too well that only a month ago he had had his voice restored to him because Leo Dupont, praying before the Holy Face, had wrested from God a complete cure! How could he dare now to raise his voice to protest against Mr. Dupont's further importunings of the Divine Majesty? With one effort he managed to crush the doubts that rose to disturb his peace. His better judgment now urged him to do but one thing, to give credit where credit was due. He realized everything here was too holy, too deep, too mysterious for him. He was a simple priest. This Leo Dupont was a prodigy. So Father Musy continued kneeling in silence, but as he knelt he knew this was one of those moments which would have to decide for him forever after on which side of an issue he would be compelled to take his stand. The priest noticed that Madame Viot and the cancer-stricken lady came from the closet, a broad smile illuminating both faces.

"Oh, thank God! One of the frightful wounds is healed," exclaimed Madame Viot.

"Kneel down and we will pray again," said Leo Dupont, without waiting, and for the eighth consecutive time the invocations before the Holy Face were recited and Miss Viot proceeded to make her eighth anointing. This time the second of the three wounds was healed.

Then for the ninth time, Leo and the group knelt down and made their petition. When Madame Viot finally finished her ninth anointing, she came forth with the patient completely cured. The third and last gaping wound was closed. The young lady, seeing herself cured, ran out into the garden, overcome with joy.[61]

Father Musy seemed speechless, though not from a throat affliction this time. He was speechless from sheer amazement, and Leo, who saw this, went up to him and said simply, "Father, with God nothing is impossible! What a contradiction it would be to think that God would create billions of

---

61 *Life of Leon Papin-Dupont*, PETER JANVIER, 1882, p. 259.

human beings out of nothing, and be unable to cure a litte sore!"

"Mr. Dupont, I've seen marvelous things in your home, here. I want to assure you that I will report all of these three cures to His Eminence, the Cardinal. Somehow, I think I am beginning to understand a little. You would want to see the Holy Face Devotion spread all over the world, am I right? But in order that this might become a reality, it will require the stimulus of a bishop to bring this about. Isn't that so? Well, I was thinking that if those who have actually received miracles through the Holy Face should make a strong effort to bring the efficacy of this Devotion to the attention of the Church authorities, who knows how successful to the cause this avalanche of petitions may prove!"

"Father, let your conscience be your guide! I am not an ecclesiastical advisor. I hold no position of rank in the Church. I am the 'pilgrim' of St. Etienne Street, as you see, privately offering some poor prayers before the Holy Face."

Father Musy realized Leo Dupont was a man not easily drawn out about himself. But he decided to try again. "I expect you might have been reproved for your zeal in this Devotion, even though you carry it on privately in your home. Is that why you are so reticent?"

"I am not free to speak," replied Leo.

"But these three miracles which I will bring to the attention of the Cardinal will certainly convince him of the efficacy of the Holy Face Cultus. I will tell my bishop about it too, and ask him to begin Devotion to the Holy Face in my parish church."

"Hold on, Father. To practice public Devotion to the Holy Face as a means of reparation would require a Brief from the Holy Father, which a bishop would first have to secure from him. I can privately have my devotions to the Holy Face, and privately I can do what I wish to advance the cause. But you as a priest must wait for the voice of authority to allow you to propagate this Work."

"You seem to be well posted on all the facts in the case. You must have met with some unhappy experiences in the past," commented Father Musy.

"I knew of two priests who wished to spread literature on Reparation to the Holy Face and to work toward inaugurating the Devotion in their parish churches, and were not allowed to do either."

"But Devotion to the Holy Face is devotion to Christ, and it has been practiced by Mary at Nazareth, and by Veronica on Calvary . . . ."

"I must check your enthusiasm to remind you that so was Devotion to the Sacred Heart practiced by Mary and by St. John the Evangelist as he leaned on the Saviour's breast. Yet when St. Margaret Mary of Alacoque was instructed by Divine Revelations to launch this worship of Christ under this special form, it took a hundred years to see her mission finally take root."

"Well, then as a layman you seem to be able to do what I as a priest cannot do."

"That's right. I can carry on my devotions at home, and people are welcome to come here to pray if they wish to do so. Let me assure you, however, that this new form of worship, the Cult of the Holy Face, has not originated with me, nor has it been my idea. It has been revealed by God to a very holy sister, of whom I cannot now speak . . . ."

"Well, I am happy that at least you, as a layman, can give impetus to this wonderful Work. Strange, the lay apostolate which proved so necessary during the recent revolutionary outbursts seems to have for its object ever higher and higher missions." Father Musy was grateful that the Church had a layman like Leo Dupont, in whose home he together with many others had received extraordinary favors. He was happy, too, that the mission of an unknown nun, to whom the Devotion of the Holy Face had been revealed, was not entirely subdued, but was even now receiving its first stimulus in the living room of this layman who styled himself a "poor pilgrim" of St. Etienne Street.

And as Father Musy spoke of the apostolate of the lay people, Leo Dupont became aware of that scene in the Sulpician Seminary many, many years ago. Faintly, Leo recalled what the Rector of the Seminary had told him that day when he learned for certain that he could not be a priest, "I think

God has some work for you to do in the world as a layman."

But Leo, unwilling to consider himself singled out for any high purpose, resolutely banished these thoughts and merely answered, "As for my part in this Work, it is only a temporary arrangement, I am sure. The day will come when the Pope will be informed of everything, and he will establish the Reparation to the Holy Face in time to yet save the world from Communistic revolutionary destruction, which is its chief aim."

Taking his leave, the priest paused at the door and whispered, "Mr. Dupont, I'll be discreet when I call on the Cardinal. Nevertheless, I will speak to him about the cures received through the Devotion to the Holy Face. We shall go in a group to the Cardinal's house this evening."

"I realize that if your conscience bids you to register your voice in favor of the New Worship, you must do it. I am asking nothing at all for myself nor even for the Devotion; but I am glad to know you will take a stand. After all, why should we waste our time talking about the weather to those with whom we should be speaking about the Church, souls, and eternity!"

At dinner that evening, Leo acquainted his mother with the incidents of the day.

"But Leo, perhaps now that three of Cardinal Morlot's friends from Paris all received miraculous cures something will be done. Who knows, maybe the Cardinal will ask the Holy Father for a Brief and begin the Devotions to the Holy Face," said Madame Arnaud, encouragingly.

"Only God knows! But still in the meantime we have our prayers to say, and our work to do."

"Yes, and not much time left to do these good works, and say these prayers!" Madame Arnaud said pensively. "I realize I am getting very old, Leo."

"But are you well, Mother?" asked Leo.

"Yes, I am fairly well, as I have ever been nearly all my life. May His Holy Name be praised! However I am beginning to feel that life is ebbing. I would so like to see the Archbishop approve Sister Marie Pierre's mission before I pass away."

Two days later Leo received a letter from the archepiscopal palace.

"Maybe it has something to do with the Devotion to the Holy Face. Maybe Father Musy's report to the Cardinal made him change his mind at last," said Madame Arnaud as she waited for Leo to announce the contents of the letter.

"You are right, Mother. Maybe this is the Cardinal's approval. Perhaps the schemes of revolutionary Communists who are plotting to . . . ." Leo stopped. It was no use any longer to anticipate a triumph. The letter was an invitation to a dinner that was scheduled at the Cardinal's palace.

"But what have I to do with attending dinner parties?" protested Leo to his mother. Then finally, giving in to her better judgment, he consented. "Well, if you think so, I'll go."

The affair called for a trip to the tailor. Leo was measured for a full dress suit, and made arrangements for a hired carriage to call for him.

Leo blended well with the other guests at the Cardinal's palace that evening, and the Cardinal looked approvingly at the gentleman from St. Etienne Street.

"Monsieur, we are happy to have you."

Leo bowed and kissed the prelate's ring.

"Father Musy was here a couple of weeks ago and told me they received three wonderful cures before the Holy Face in your home."

"Your Grace, the favors continue unabated," replied Leo.

As more guests arrived, the Cardinal with his accustomed ease, went from guest to guest, and Leo, looking on, began to wonder after all, why he came.

Presently, a visitor from Paris was announced and on being introduced to Leo, he said, "Ah, so you are the celebrated thaumaturgist! Everybody in Paris knows about you. As for myself, Father Musy personally related to me the full story of his cure." Then, adjusting his monocle, he said with an amused smile, "Now the fact that Father Musy can relate anything at all speaks in itself very highly of your curative powers, for I knew him to be speechless for four long years. You see, I ought to know, I am his physician."

Leo made no answer, and the doctor continued, "Our Cardinal is highly impressed with the cures that take place in your home."

"Is he?" came from Leo, hopelessly. Just then dinner was announced and the guests went up the wide carpeted staircase to the dining hall on the second floor. Familiarly, the guests began making themselves at home around the large table. Leo suddenly noticed that all the places were taken, while he alone remained standing. Through an oversight one plate was missing. A servant began to apologize to Leo.

"I'm sorry, but somehow . . . ." he stammered, not knowing just what to do for the moment. It was an impossible situation! A guest in the Cardinal's dining room and there was no place for him!

Before the servant had a chance to rectify the awkward mistake, Leo was at the Archbishop's elbow, saying, "Your Eminence, you see now that I ought not to dine with persons of high rank since there is no place for me. . . ."

"But, but," stuttered the Cardinal, as he turned to catch the attention of the headwaiter, to demand that a place at the table be provided at once. However, he was too late. Leo had already made his way downstairs and before anyone realized what had happened, he was out in the street, walking quickly past rows of buildings in search of a cab to take him back to the Rue St. Etienne, where he felt he belonged.[62]

---

62 *Ibid.*, p. 336.

23

On days when there were not too many visitors seeking a favor from the Holy Face in Leo's parlor, he was busy making arrangements for a better and more efficient method of helping the poor of Tours.

"St. Vincent's gives away clothing," he told his mother, "but often the clothing we give is so soiled and torn that the poor can't use it. I would like to see the clothing department as a unit, separate from St. Vincent's. In that way, we could attend efficiently to providing clean and mended clothes for the needy."

"How would you run this clothing society?" asked his mother.

"I would call for volunteers who would offer their services to clean and mend clothes before it is given away. What kind of charity is it to give people dirty rags!"

"Leo, go ahead and organize your clothing society," agreed Madame Arnaud at once. "I will be the first to offer my services to sew anything you want. I can still use the needle, and I like to keep my hands busy," she said. Now past seventy-five, but still alert, she was always anxious for some light activity.

"If we find we cannot get enough volunteers, I suggest we hire a few people, and pay them a wage for their services. But by all means let us provide decent clothing," Leo went on. "The revolutionists are inciting people more and more. It is up to us to voluntarily help our poor. It is the obligation of those Christians who have more, to help those who have less. By doing this, we can avoid a catastrophe, and also fulfill the law of God."

The society was formed. It was to be dedicated to St. Martin, the famous miracle worker of 11th century Tours, whom Leo so much honored and whom he also very much resembled. St. Martin was known for his charity to the poor and Leo, who had already expended more than half of his large fortune helping orphanages, schools, homes for the aged, and convents, was unable to hide his good works. Moreover, St. Martin became famous for the astounding miracles granted through his intercession during his lifetime, and now Leo Dupont, in his parlor on St. Etienne Street, was so instrumental in wresting miracles from Heaven that his reputation as a thaumaturgist had crossed the boundaries of his own country, and spread to foreign lands and across oceans.

Noting the progress of the new society, Leo wrote to a friend, "During the past four months we have distributed 300 new garments. Our society has also received legacies which prove that rich persons are pleased to find a means of assisting the poor."

Then, to his mother one evening, Leo began to relate another project that he was thinking about lately. "You know, we now have a St. Martin's Clothing Society here in Tours, but there is still no St. Martin's Church in Tours! Twenty years we have lived here, yes, twenty years have passed since the old vegetable woman told me about the place where St. Martin's tomb rests beneath the earth's surface, and I who thought that something could and should have been done to repair the destruction of St. Martin's Basilica by the revolutionists, have learned since how slowly progress the works of religion!"

That evening the members of St. Martin's Clothing Society met at Leo's home for their usual monthly meeting, for Leo had been elected President in spite of his protests. Before the meeting adjourned, Leo decided to make a suggestion. "Reverend Father, and esteemed members, we are but few, yet is seems to me we could try to make some effort toward a possible rebuilding of the Basilica of St. Martin."

The committee and the priest looked at Leo with astonishment, wondering what he would attempt next. It was one thing to form a St. Martin's Clothing Society and another thing to rebuild a Basilica!

But Leo soon proved to them the reasonableness of his suggestion. "I do not propose that we can do it with our bare hands. I only propose that we draw up a petition to consider the reconstruction of St. Martin's Church at some future date and that we ask a blessing on this work. I admit that this would be a very small beginning, but it would be something."

Leo's resolution was approved. The first step to rebuild famous St. Martin's had at last been taken. Thereafter, at successive meetings of St. Martin's Clothing Society, the members consulted as to how the project could be launched. Finally, Leo and the moderator, Father Verdier, had drawn up a strategic plan. Since Cardinal Morlot was scheduled to celebrate Mass for St. Martin's Clothing Society on November 11, the feast of St. Martin, it seemed the right occasion to bring the subject to the attention of the prelate.

This was to be attempted by Father Verdier in the course of his sermon. "The Board of St. Martin's Clothing Society, in whose name I speak, would wish to see collected the scattered stones of the Basilica of St. Martin, and to restore to the veneration of the faithful the great thaumaturgist of Gaul . . . ." It was out. And Cardinal Morlot, who listened attentively to the sermon, realized that this group of laymen were resolved to act. When, that same year, the Holy Father was asked to bless the project, he did so willingly.

"Do you think, Leo, that I will live to see the day when they begin to excavate?" asked Madame Arnaud.

"I hope you live to see the day when they actually find the tomb where the relics of St. Martin are buried," said Leo encouragingly.

Adele, stepping into the room, announced a visit from Father Pasquier.

"News has just reached us at the rectory that the Archbishop of Paris has been murdered!"

"Cardinal Sibour murdered?" Leo shook his head.

"Yes," replied the priest, "and may God forgive us for this outrage committed in Catholic France!"

A few weeks later, Cardinal Morlot of Tours was appointed the new Archbishop of Paris, and Tours waited for a new ordinary. He was none other than Monsignor Guibert, Cardinal Morlot's secretary.[63]

"Leo, do you think the new bishop might promote the Work of the Holy Face?" asked Madame Arnaud, confidentially.

"No, Mother, I don't think he will. I am sorry to disappoint you but, you see, Bishop Guibert was Cardinal Morlot's former secretary and official advisor, his first man, so to say. I am inclined to believe Cardinal Morlot might have endorsed Sister Marie Pierre's mission, if he had had a different counselor. My opinion is that Bishop Guibert will keep the archives containing the writings of Sister Marie Pierre sealed more tightly than his predecessor ever did."

Leo's words came true to the letter. But in the meantime, the work of restoring St. Martin's Church, once begun, went on. Mr. Ratel, who was chief engineer for the railroad, and therefore a man well capable of conducting the research which would establish beyond a doubt the precise location of the Basilica and the tomb, met frequently with Leo for discussions. Title to the lands and buildings calculated to be in the vicinity where St. Martin's once stood was acquired by the diocese in less than two years. The engineers were now ready with their sketches, and excavations were begun. Digging went on month after month, as the superintendent worked feverishly to come upon some trace of the foundations that once held up the ancient walls of the celebrated Church.

As they dug beneath the cellars of some of the homes, they came upon two small parallel walls of white gravel-stone, which the superintendent analyzed as the sides of the vault of the sepulcher in which reposed the remains of St. Martin. More engineers were consulted and excavations were halted.

The tomb of St. Martin was found, beyond a doubt.[64] It was the year 1860. Leo could not tear himself away from

---

63 *Ibid.*, pp. 172, 173.
64 *Ibid.*, p. 185.

the sacred spot. When he finally arrived at home that evening to give his mother the good news, it was almost midnight. "Rejoice, Mother. We have found the tomb of St. Martin. It is ours. We have it at last!"

"So I really lived to see the happy day," she said contentedly.

"But wait until I tell you where we found it!"

"Where, Leo, did you find it?"

"Just where the old vegetable woman told me it was more than twenty-five years ago! We found the tomb beneath a cellar of one of the houses raised over it, and not under the public street, where the revolutionaries had planned to bury it. Their plans had miscarried. No wagons ever rode over St. Martin's tomb, Mother, and no horses' hoofs ever beat upon it! The vegetable vendor was right—she was right! The tomb was not under the public street."

A small oratory was at once raised over the spot. An altar was erected, and a space cleared to accommodate the hundreds who came to venerate the relics of the glorious St. Martin and the many priests who came to offer the Sacrifice of the Mass.

A month later, Madame Arnaud, old but always in good health, took ill, and a few days later was on the point of death. Having received the last Sacraments, she said to her son, "Leo, all during my life I have feared to die. But now something wonderful has happened to me. I am altogether happy and even glad to go. I want to see my Creator. Leo, this is a wonderful grace."

"I am happy to know it, Mother," answered Leo, sympathetically, "because I have come to tell you that you shall soon enter upon your agony."

"You mean, I am about to die?"

"Yes, Mother. Perhaps within the hour . . . ."

A short while later, after an agony that lasted only sixty seconds, Madame Arnaud fell asleep in the Lord, at the age of eighty-two years.

24

THREE YEARS later, in 1863, a temporary church to accommodate 1,500 people was built on the spot of St. Martin's tomb. Though there were no resources to plan at once the erection of a costly Basilica, there was now a temporary church in the city of Tours dedicated to the memory of St. Martin.

But Leo and his friends were growing old. Father Pasquier, Leo's confessor for many years, was unable to get around, and Leo with the customary respect he always had for his spiritual father, would call regularly with a hired carriage to take the aged priest on some errand, or out for a drive. On occasions when the priest would go inside some house to call, Leo could be seen outdoors, watching the horse at the curb as if he were an ordinary driver.

"There is a pilgrimage to Paray le Monial, and friends are urging me to come along with them," said Leo to the priest as they rode in the carriage one day. "But, Father Pasquier, I can't go. The Sacred Heart will understand. My rheumatism is bothering me again. As it is not Our Lord's will to cure me, I must make a trip to the baths again to seek some natural remedies."

Adele decided to take advantage of Leo's absence from home. "Mr. Dupont, the house needs refurnishing, and I would like your permission to attend to a few things here . . . ."

"You're right, Adele. Since my mother died, I've let things drift. Do whatever you think is right, and needs attention."

Adele took full advantage of her master's absence. For some time, owing to his gout, Leo had moved an iron bedstead down to the parlor, concealing it from view with draperies.

To Adele this arrangement was displeasing since it detracted from the appearance of the large fine drawing room that opened out into the garden.

Upon his return home, Leo was pleased with the many improvements. "You have done very well, Adele, and everything looks fine. But what have you done with my iron bed?" he asked.

"I moved it upstairs, sir, where it always used to be until you got this idea of the curtain and the bedstead in the parlor."

"But the bedstead was concealed with a curtain. You see, with my gout, it is easier for me to get around on the first floor. Besides, I was able that way to spend both the day and the night before the Image of the Holy Face."

"You will excuse me, sir, but if I may suggest, you have a very nice small picture of the Holy Face, which you can keep upstairs. As for a bedstead in the parlor, it didn't look right."

"But Adele, the bedstead was closed in with a curtain during the day," objected Leo.

"Yes, but you are growing more feeble month after month, and the time will soon be here when you will have to keep to your bed in the daytime, and then the curtain will not avail. Visitors will come to pray before the Holy Face in the parlor, and you who will perhaps be ill in bed will be continuously disturbed. God does not want that!"

"I suppose you are right, Adele. But I can hardly become reconciled as to why this had to be done."

"I did what was best, sir. I feel I have charge of you. There is no one else but myself and I must see to your comfort, as Madame would have wanted me to do had she lived." After a short pause, she added, "I suppose we must all make little sacrifices once in a while."

A couple of weeks later, Leo sat in his room in front of a blazing fire, warming a painful rheumatic leg while he read his breviary. Adele knocked at his door, not with her usual gentle knock but a bit impatiently.

Asked to come in, Adele at once came to the point. "Mr.

Dupont, the portrait I had of you hanging in my room over the fireplace is missing. Did you take it?"

"What do you want with an old portrait of mine? You have the true portrait of our Blessed Lord downstairs, His Own Holy Face. What else do you need?"

"I'm serious, Mr. Dupont. I want that portrait back," she said beginning to fear the worst. "Tell me where it is?"

Leo pointed towards the brightly blazing fire in his chimney. Adele paled. Looking into the chimney she recognized one right angle of the familiar heavy, hand-carved frame. All else was in ashes.

"Oh, you burned the portrait! How could you do such a thing! It was the only portrait we ever had of you." Weeping, Adele fled from the room.

But Leo, rubbing his hands vigorously, perhaps for the first time in his life laughed while another wept. If little sacrifices were good for him, no doubt, they were also good for Adele Colombe. And so passed out of existence the only genuine portrait of Leo Dupont. Could anything be more fitting than this, that Leo who was destined to leave men the lesson of adoring Christ's own portrait, should have consigned his own to a heap of ashes in the chimney?[65]

Leo was now sixty-eight. He spent almost all his time in the parlor before the Image of the Holy Face. Visitors still came to his house, some days crowding his parlor, other days trickling in smaller numbers. Requests for pictures of the Holy Face and for vials of the holy oil from his lamp continued unabated.

But perhaps among the many who came seeking cures and other favors, only a few noticed the Bible on Leo's reading desk, or attached to it any vital importance. Yet this one volume was to Leo the well of all his inspiration and progress in the knowledge and science of God. Leo loved to compare the Old Testament with the New, and to observe how passages from the one threw light upon the other. He also drew from the Scriptures wonderful analogies and coincidents which he applied to the events of the day. Not content

---

65 *Ibid.*, p. 408.

to study Sacred Writ by himself and to interpret it in the traditional Catholic way, he went deeper and sought assistance to better understand the Sacred Text from a distinguished priest and scholar, Father Allouard, who had a standing Sunday evening invitation to his table.

Leo's letters at this time reach a climax of deep faith. When commenting on Sacred Scripture, he revealed the source of his interior strength. On March 29, 1865, writing to an intimate friend, he said, "Today when I placed for the first time a lamp before the Holy Bible, I remarked the appropriateness of the words of the 118th Psalm, 'I entreated Thy Face with all my heart; have mercy on me according to Thy word.' The lamp is at the corner of my bureau, facing my large Bible and I, miserable creature, am between the two lights in reparation for blasphemy. For a long time I had thought of placing a lamp before the Word of God to pay it homage, and you are the first to whom I have mentioned it."

The Abbe Janvier, Dean of the Metropolitan Chapter of Tours, who knew Leo well for many years, and later became his biographer, remarking on his deep veneration of the Bible, said, "Of all the great lovers of Holy Scripture, Leo Dupont is the first, so far as it is known, whose devotion has induced him to honor it like the Blessed Sacrament, by keeping a lamp before it day and night . . . ."[66]

"Leo Dupont wished ever to expiate the crime of blasphemy daily committed by the unbelieving, and by ignorant Christians, who deny the divine inspiration of our Holy Bible and see in it mere human and ordinary utterances. 'Scripture,' he said, 'is the Face of God; before that Face, as before the Holy Face, the fire ought to burn day and night. I see Jesus Christ whole and entire in each word of the Bible. Jesus Christ cannot be divided.' "[67]

But if there were many who looked at Leo with reverence and esteem, there were also those who sought an opportunity to embarrass him. One day, an old friend called on Leo, bringing with him a lady whom Leo had never met.

---

66 *Ibid.*, p. 224.
67 *Ibid.*, p. 224.

"I see that your parlor has become a sort of museum, where one can behold every sort of crutch, cane, and brace imaginable. I have taken the liberty to bring with me a visitor who is anxious to meet you."

He introduced the lady, and then Leo said, "Yes, Gaston, people leave their crutches here as mementos of their cure. They come before the Holy Face maimed and crippled, supported on these instruments of torture. They leave the Holy Face a short while later, walking securely on their feet."

"Is there as great a concourse of people as ever?"

"No, there are fewer callers, yet would you believe that between January and April of this year, I have received fifty-two certificates of favors obtained through the unctions with the holy oil?"

"Do these certificates reach you by mail?" asked the lady visitor.

Leo replied in the affirmative.

"That means people receive cures and extraordinary favors through Devotion to the Holy Face without coming here?"

"Yes, they do, for that is precisely what the signed certificates which are sent to me attest."

"How is it done?" the lady pursued.

"Persons living away from Tours simply make a Novena to the Holy Face, or they recite the Litany composed by Sister Marie Pierre, and then make the anointing with the holy oil from the lamp . . . ."

"Do they procure novena leaflets and the oil from you?"

"Yes," modestly admitted Leo.

"Then, in that case, the only actual part you play in these miraculous cures is that you supply and pay for the oil!" the lady concluded.

"You are right, Madame. That's all I do. I only pay for the oil. The good God does all the rest. I marvel how well you understand it. I wish you could explain this matter to others who seem to have the idea that some merit of mine attaches to the favors granted."

But had the lady pursued her calculations to a final conclusion, to determine how much exactly had Leo paid for the oil he had distributed during the past fifteen years, she would have had reason to believe that this one charity alone could have singled out Leo Dupont for unique distinctions. Since 1851, Leo had distributed personally or through the mails approximately one million vials of oil. Estimating one vial to cost merely two cents, Leo Dupont had spent about $20,000 for the vials of oil he distributed free of charge, a considerable charity in itself.

But did he pay only for the oil? Leo's physician knew Leo paid much more in his health. His home had become a veritable clinic where he was exposed to disease day in and day out. He was compelled to anoint ulcers, and to look at gaping wounds that would have made a lesser man reel with nausea. His life became an endless contact with ailing incurables whom doctors sent away as hopeless cases. What other refined person in good circumstances would condescend to endless commerce with victims of diseases, in the last stages of disintegration? Yet, Leo not only accepted them, but he invited them into his parlor, knelt with them, prayed with them, and anointed their sores tirelessly during a span that had stretched now for fifteen years.

Because of the large number of extraordinary cures, there also devolved on him the burden of a tremendous correspondence. Unwilling to leave anything unfinished, and always secretly hoping that these marvelous favors from the Holy Face might some day incline the Church authorities to make known the life and revelations of Sister Marie Pierre, Leo Dupont felt it as his responsibility to keep a written account of favors obtained, and to provide safe deposit for the numerous testimonials and certificates sent to him. The Devotion to the Holy Face had become for him a full-time career.

There were those who at times wanted to make some financial contribution toward advancing the Work of Reparation, particularly those who had received extraordinary favors in Leo's home.

"We would like to leave a donation, as a pledge of our gratitude," some would say. "You could use the money to spread Devotion to the Holy Face."

"But no one is allowed to spread Devotion to the Holy

Face. It must first be approved by Rome, through the ordinary ecclesiastical channels. So you see, I have no need for your contribution," Leo would answer.

"But what about the Devotion to the Holy Face right here in your home?"

"Ah, gentlemen, that is strictly a private affair. It does not call for any heavy financial backing. I am in no need of financial help in order to keep a small light burning before the Image of the Holy Face."

"Then, at least, accept our money and use it for the poor . . . ."

"There are poor-boxes in every church in Tours. I suggest you deposit your offerings there. It will be sure to reach the needy without my acting as agent . . . ."

Leo was still the lawyer. But essentially he was a saint. If visitors wanted the gratifying sensation of leaving an offering, nothing would have given them greater satisfaction than leaving it in Mr. Dupont's home. When they were told by Leo to drop their dollar bills secretly into a hidden poor-box in the darkened corner of some church, their almsgiving somehow lost the glitter that too many of them demanded from their acts of giving.

During the next two years, Leo suffered serious recurrent spells of rheumatism so that he was no longer able to attend to parlor calls, but was compelled to spend much time in his room on the second floor. He now hired a servant whom he trained to receive the various visitors who still came to his home to seek favors through prayers to the Holy Face. The servant would escort them to the miraculous picture and supply leaflets and vials of oil when these were requested.

"Mr. Dupont, a gentleman who says he knows you very well is here and would appreciate a personal visit. His name is Mr. Vilmote. I told him you were not very well . . . ."

"I am much better today, Adele. Help me into the chair and ask Mr. Vilmote to come upstairs."

No time was lost discussing trifles in Leo's upstairs apartment. "Of course, visitors still come, but it is not as it used to be. There is a marked decline," Leo was saying to his friend.

"This must be a disappointment to you."

"Oh, no. God knows that my old age would not permit greater exertions. One man can do only so much and no more."

"Then you think that your mission relative to the Work of the Holy Face is about fulfilled?" asked Mr. Vilmote.

"My dear friend, you are one of the few who know all the facts. Then you ought to realize that the mission of the Holy Face Devotion was not entrusted to me, a poor layman, but to a cloistered nun to whom our Lord said: *And, indeed, to whom shall I reveal the power of My Holy Face if not to a Carmelite whose duty it is to consume her life in contemplation of Me?* It is Sister's mission, sir, and I am but her poor servant . . . ."

"Well, then, how do matters look for the Sister's mission?"

"If you want the plain facts, then here they are. We are as far away from the establishment of the Reparation through Devotion to the Holy Face as we ever were!"

"How is that?"

"Our Lord demanded that a Brief authorizing a Confraternity dedicated to the Work be secured from Rome through the Archbishop of Tours, so the project would have a solid foundation."

"And there is no Brief?"

"My dear Vilmote, indeed there is no Brief! Cardinal Morlot had sealed the Sister's writings and placed an interdict upon them. His successor, who was his former secretary, continues the censure."

"In spite of all the miracles which have been worked here in your house for nearly seventeen years?" asked Mr. Vilmote.

"In spite of them!" replied Leo.

"It looks hopeless . . . ."

"Don't say that. Never say that!"

"But how can you continue to hope after all these years, when two successive archbishops continue to keep the Sister's mission sealed up in secrecy. It looks to me like a one-man institution. You are that one man!"

"Too many people have received favors and miracles through the Holy Face, my dear friend, for me to think that

I am the only man interested in the adoration of His Sacred Countenance . . . ."

"But you are the only person who is carrying on the Work, doing something for it," objected Mr. Vilmote. "You must face facts, Leo. You are getting very old, and if you should die, what will happen to the Devotion to the Holy Face?"

Leo thought of a number of answers he could give his friend, but he only smiled, and said nothing.

25

THE FOLLOWING year, 1868, found Leo somewhat improved in health. He was able, for several weeks without interruption, to make his way to his favorite place of worship, the Chapel of the Discalced Carmelites on Ursuline Street, where he went early every morning at half past five to hear Mass and to receive Holy Communion.

One morning on his way out of the Chapel, when he paused as usual over the holy water stoup, there to whisper a few extra words of prayer, he heard a voice at his side. It was a priest.

"Mr. Dupont, if you have a few moments, I would like to speak with you . . . ."

"But, it seems to me, I do not recognize you, Father," Leo said, as the two walked out into the sunshine.

"No, I don't suppose you would be expected to recognize me because, you see, we never met." The two smiled at each other. "But that does not mean I do not know you, sir, for the fact is I know you so well that I know why you stood lingering so long over the holy water stoup a moment ago . . . ."

"You know even that secret?" Leo asked, wistfully.

"Yes, I know the secret. Sister Marie Pierre is buried beneath the chapel, in the vicinity of the holy water stoup, and so each time you leave the Carmelite Chapel, you stop to pray a moment at the tomb of your favorite saint . . . ."

"Yes, Father, you know the full secret. Though the Sister is unknown, she is my favorite saint!"

"As for me, I am indebted to Father Musy for acquainting me with the facts concerning Devotion to the Holy Face in

Tours. I don't know if you remember him, but Father Musy received an instantaneous cure in your parlor some years back. He regained the use of his voice."

"I remember Father Musy very well," Leo answered. How could he ever forget? Three miracles were granted, one to Father Musy, one to his mother, and one to his acquaintance who came from Paris to seek the favors. Being friends of Cardinal Morlot, who sent them, Leo had hoped the triple wonders would win over the prelate to the cause of the Holy Face. But that was nearly twenty-five years ago. Since then, Leo's files were swelled to overflowing with testimonials from all over the world, attesting to the power of the Holy Face Devotion. But all this favorable evidence had failed to win official approval.

"It might interest you to know," continued the priest, "that Father Musy was fortunate enough to procure some years ago a copy of the booklet *Abridgement of Facts* from which we both learned the details of Sister Marie Pierre's revelations."

"Yes, I recall the little booklet, tediously written by hand, and of which there were only fifty copies in circulation . . . ."

"And has nothing more ever been published about the nun?"

"Nothing," replied Leo.

"Yet, the diocesan authorities must have held Sister Marie Pierre in deep veneration, or else they would not have allowed her remains to be buried beneath the chapel?" logically pressed the priest.

"Well, since you are so interested, I will be happy to tell you something about that. But first let me invite you to my home for some breakfast."

An hour later, seated in Leo's house on the Rue St. Etienne, conversing about the many wonders that took place there, the priest said, "But you promised to tell me how it came about that the body of Sister Marie Pierre was transferred from the cemetery to the convent grounds. When did it happen?"

"It happened about thirteen years ago. The city authorities, I learned, were in the process of moving the old cemetery farther outside the city limits. I became terribly worried that the grave of Sister Marie Pierre might be lost to posterity forever. I felt it was up to me to do my utmost to prevent such a misfortune. So I pleaded with the bishop to allow me to exhume the remains of Sister Marie Pierre and to have them buried under the floor of the monastery."

"How long had Sister been dead at the time?"

"Seven years," replied Leo.

"And the diocesan authorities gave you their consent?"

"Yes, they did."

"Quite a rare privilege!"

"Indeed! But Sister Marie Pierre deserved it."

"Yes, and she deserves much more, and will get much more some day."

"And when that happens, the world will be the better for it. Sister Marie Pierre has a timely cure for the ills of our day." Then, rising, Leo added, "But come, Father, let me show you the picture of the Holy Face in my parlor."

"So this is the miracle room!" exclaimed the priest as the Image of the Saviour's Face came into view.

Both knelt and prayed a while, and then the priest broached another topic, "Mr. Dupont, I have just returned from Lourdes. Have you been there yet?"

"No, I have not. However, since the apparition of our Lady to Bernadette, ten years ago, I have managed to keep myself well informed on all the wonders that have taken place at the holy mountain. In the meantime, I felt my place was here in this shrine of the Holy Face, which so many people have been visiting . . . ."

"There is no doubt about it. You belong here," answered the priest.

"But since you've just come from Lourdes, you must have news of developments there."

"Yes, I have. The chapel the Lady told Bernadette she wished to have built, already stands as a glorious reality. It has only recently been opened to the public."

Leo sighed. The priest, pulling up his chair closer to Mr. Dupont, as if in a gesture to make a special confidence, said, "Mr. Dupont, tell me, how do you feel about the success of

Bernadette? Although she received the mission to ask for the erection of a church to Mary's honor while she was only a girl of fourteen, yet she accomplished the great work in less than eight years."

"Eight years? Why Bernadette had her bishop's full consent in less than two years. Bishop Laurence almost instantly did everything the Lady enjoined in her message to Bernadette."

"Why does not Sister Marie Pierre, who received her mission to establish Holy Face Devotion as a means of Reparation, succeed after a lapse of so many years?"

"Would you expect me to be able to explain to you the hidden designs of God?"

"No, but just humanly speaking, it appears to me as a strange contradiction. A simple child in the world says she had apparitions of Mary for two short weeks and promptly succeeds in convincing her bishop. On the other hand, a cloistered nun with vows has revelations stretching over more than five years, she dies in the odor of sanctity, she is granted the privilege of burial under the monastery chapel, and yet, now nearly twenty-five years after her death, her life and revelations are consigned to the archives. Nobody is allowed to mention the mission of Sister Marie Pierre!"

"There is much truth in what you say, but, Father, I believe that Bernadette had her full share of grief and sorrow in bringing about the fulfillment of her mission. Besides, she still continues to suffer poor health and unbelievable humiliations in her convent."

"True, but she saw the realization of her mission. Devotions and processions at Lourdes are the routine of the day."

"That's splendid!" replied Leo.

"But what about your Work here? Are you not disappointed with the delays and obstacles that you meet? Especially when you see Lourdes so triumphant?"

"No, Father, Lourdes has been my greatest consolation. When I see Our Lady parceling out favors to her children at the Grotto, I say to myself, 'Patience, she will yet bring men to kneel before the Holy Face in due time.' For, indeed, what greater desire does Mary have than this, that all men should acknowledge and worship her Divine Son? So when Our Lady through her sweet apparitions at Lourdes shall have persuaded her children to say the rosary, they will then become prepared to kneel before the Face of Jesus."

"I never thought of it that way," answered the priest, with surprise.

"Let me confide something more to you. When I witnessed the indifference and opposition to the Work of the Holy Face, I was at first bewildered, especially since so many miracles had attested to its power. Eventually I came to the conclusion that the world was not yet ready for this Devotion. For you see, my friend, Devotion to the Holy Face is the highest and most exalted worship there could be since its aim is to adore the Triune God, Himself. In the Face of Christ we see mirrored the very attributes of the Blessed Trinity as well as His human perfections. When we pray to the Sacred Heart of Jesus we are essentially concerned with His Humanity, but, I repeat, when we look on the Holy Face we are concerned with the Divinity, for 'the Head of Christ is God,' as St. Paul says."

The priest said nothing but only nodded reverentially.

"Let us recall that passage from Scripture which says that 'Wisdom had built herself a house.' How simple for us to grasp that the Head of Christ is that House which Wisdom had built herself. Noting, therefore, how exalted is Devotion to the Holy Face, should it be any wonder to us then that we might be obliged to wait a hundred years to see it become a reality?"

"A hundred years is a long time," replied the priest. "After all you've done to promote the Work, are you resigned to die without seeing it accomplished?"

"But, of course, I am! After I'm gone there will be others better fitted than I am to carry on."

"But to have worked without seeing the fruits is a discouraging ordeal. Few would have any patience or taste for it. We teach a class and see the graduates. We plant a seed and reap a harvest. Yet, you are satisfied to die without seeing your efforts bring any reward."

"But I have seen many of my works crowned with visible

success, Father. For, you see, I've given my time to other projects such as renovating churches, founding an old people's home, helping the orphanage—all of which has been a source of deep satisfaction to me. But, now that you mentioned this, I realize that there was someone who had been completely deprived of all such satisfaction . . . ."

"You mean Sister Marie Pierre?"

"Yes, I allude to her. She lived a life of prayer and penance inside a cloister and although she spent herself pleading and praying for the accomplishment of a mission the Saviour had entrusted to her, she died without seeing any fruits. Humanly speaking, she failed completely. But did she despair? To the contrary, she died hoping that God would crown the Work when he willed, realizing that God's plans, though intercepted for a time, can never ultimately miscarry, because His Will is supreme."

"It has always been the way of the saints to know how to explain everything. They can wait a century or longer for what they want, and without impatience."

"Because they know that what they want is worth waiting for," replied Leo. "Sister Marie Pierre, for example, after five years of Divine revelations concerning the worship of the Holy Face, understood completely the scope of the Work of Reparation. The Face of Christ was intended to change the face of the earth. She envisioned every diocese organizing the Reparation. She saw every parish holding Sunday Devotions in honor of the Holy Face to repair for the crimes of atheism and the profanation of holy days. She saw every family exposing in their homes a picture of the Redeemer's Sacred Face, as a symbol of their faith. It was to be a new world of peace, first with God, and then with neighbor."

"If only more of us could be made to understand the meaning of the Work in that light!"

"Then we would not mind waiting even a century!" concluded Leo, with a smile. Then, noticing the clock on the mantelpiece, he added, "But while we're waiting, we could say some prayers to hurry it along. I see it is eight o'clock and time for me to begin my Little Hours . . . ."

"Do you say the Divine Office every day?" asked the priest.

Leo only nodded, after which both the host and the visitor buried themselves in the leather-covered pages of their Breviaries.

A short while later, the priest, looking up, noticed three visitors enter the living room where hung the picture of the Holy Face. Turning to Leo, the priest looked at him inquiringly, expecting he would go to see about the wishes of his three visitors. But Leo, undisturbed, continued to read his Breviary, while the visitors went to kneel before the Sacred Image, prayed for a while, then rose and walked away. Again another group of visitors came in, and repeated the same ritual, while Leo remained buried in the psalms of the Office.

The priest felt he had never seen anything like it before, as in truth he had not. But then this was the famous house on St. Etienne Street where miracles were the order of the day. The host could not be expected to be impressed if a visitor entered the house to pray before an Image of Christ, known the world over for its miraculous powers. The house on St. Etienne Street was unlike anything, for it belonged to a private citizen who found himself the custodian of a public worship.

As the priest thought about these things, he noticed a young girl being carried in. She was unable to walk. Her foot had been severely crushed, and was so swollen she could not take a step. After setting her down before the picture of the Holy Face, her family knelt to recite the celebrated Litany of the Holy Face.

The girl suddenly cried out, "My God, if it be Thy will, you can grant me a cure . . . ."

"That is not the way to pray. . . ." came from someone across the room. It was Leo, looking up from his Breviary.

"If I do not pray in the right manner, please tell me how I should do it . . . ." pleaded the invalid.

Leo put down his prayerbook, and came forward. The visiting priest also closed his Breviary.

"Child, you should pray with confidence," Leo told the girl, "and make your desire known to God in a positive manner. You should say to the Lord: 'Lord, cure me.' "

"But I can't do that! I can't make demands upon God," the invalid said humbly.

"You do not know what real prayer is, my child. You come here but all along you doubt that God will hear you. You lack trust in God. And you pretend to yourself that this is a form of respect which you have for the Almighty. When we pray, we must have a boundless confidence."

"But it seems to me that I do have faith, sir," answered the girl.

After the prayers and anointings were completed, the girl found she was able to walk, but not without pain.

"The invalid who was carried in, walked out by her own strength," said the priest to Leo, when the group had gone.

"It was not a complete cure," replied Leo in a matter-of-fact way, as he resumed the prayers he had interrupted.

An hour later, the same girl, together with her family, was back again.

"Mr. Dupont, although I am much improved, I realize you were right when you said I lacked trust. I came back to ask God for a complete cure."

After the invocations and the anointing, the girl rose, instantly and permanently cured.[68]

It was late in the afternoon when the visiting priest finally took leave of Leo. "I'll never forget the things I saw here today . . . ."

"Cures are only a small part of the favors to be obtained by all who seek them before the Face of the Lord."

"But I think these cures are astonishing," said the priest.

"Not at all! It would be more astonishing if prayers were not answered," replied Leo.[69]

---

68 *Ibid.*, p. 286.
69 *Ibid.*, p. 246.

26

THE YEAR 1870 came, and with it the Franco-Prussian War. Leo, who was utterly heartsick over his country's inability to stave off the German invader, often thought of Sister Marie Pierre who had predicted grave calamities if Reparation were not offered. Leo kept his house open day and night for soldiers to come in at any hour to pray. A hired servant was at hand to receive callers at all hours. Devotions to the Holy Face went on, and Leo now prayed as humbled Frenchmen had to pray while they submitted to a conquering invader. In his own house on the Rue St. Etienne, fifteen Prussians were quartered. Thirteen of them were Catholics and two were Protestants. Leo was grateful, however, to note that their conduct in his house was above reproach.

Meanwhile, in another part of France, at Nevers, where Bernadette, the seeress of Lourdes, was stationed as a nun, the armies of occupation were about to storm the city. The French general, greatly perturbed, approached Bernadette.

"Are you not alarmed, Sister?" he asked, gravely concerned.

"Sir, I fear only bad Catholics!" she replied.

Bernadette at Nevers and Leo Dupont at Tours both knew the war could have been averted. Where was the penance Mary demanded at the grotto in Lourdes? Where was the Reparation to the Holy Face the Saviour had exacted in the Monastery of Carmel? Was it easier to obtain the miraculous cure of a cancer, or to avert an impending war? Prayers and penance would have secured both. The bloodshed of war on French soil seemed so unnecessary. Mary merely wanted the Rosary daily, and the Saviour but asked that Sunday be sanctified by a few prayers of Reparation in addition to the obligatory morning Mass.

At the end of a year of war, France's mighty armies were defeated. Paris was besieged, and the French were compelled to surrender to the Prussians. By the terms of peace, France lost her provinces of Alsace and Lorraine, had to allow her capital to be occupied by German troops, and in addition had to pay one billion dollars in indemnities. Worse was the penalty in human suffering. Thousands lay crippled and maimed in hospitals; other thousands lay buried in their graves.

Leo did not enter into political disputes in his day, but kept himself aloof, content to be of service to his countrymen in a much higher way. Nevertheless, when it was a matter of fervent Catholics contending with the revolutionary elements for a fair election, Leo would write to them: "Be brave. Fear not the multitude of your enemies, for the battle is not yours but God's."

AT this time, the diocese of Tours was again to have a new bishop. Cardinal Guibert, the bishop of Tours for fourteen years, was promoted to the See of Paris, to succeed Cardinal Morlot, who had just passed away.

"How short is life, even when men live to a ripe old age, as did Cardinal Morlot," observed Leo when he heard the news of the recent changes. He could speak from experience in this regard, for he was now an old man himself, being nearly seventy-five.

A few days after Bishop Fruchaud had been installed as the Ordinary of Tours, Adele came to Leo with a question. "Sir, I was wondering, do you think the new bishop might approve the revelations of Sister Marie Pierre, and that, perhaps, now at last her life will become known to the world?"

"Adele, we are so old now that we can do nothing but pray, and be resigned. God does not expect anything more. Whatever the new bishop does or does not, cannot alter our poor lives in the least bit."

"But you would be happy, sir, if you knew that your favorite heroine, Sister Marie Pierre, were known to the world! It would mean so much to souls! The whole world ought to embrace this devotion!"

"It will, some day! Whoever the bishop will be, he will surely come some day, Adele, and he will light the candle which we kept flickering before the Holy Face these past years, and the candle will blaze out with a mighty brilliance, and the light of that candle will scatter all the darkness and gloom, and the world will have new hope . . . ."

"Oh, if it only were so!"

"And what is more, my dear, when that happy day dawns, then the light of that candle will become the spark of a chain reaction, spreading, going from one to another, and no power on earth will extinguish it!"

"You are that certain, sir?"

"Yes, because the Saviour promised this to Sister Marie Pierre when He said: *There is about to dawn the most beautiful work under the sun!*"

"Yes, I know," replied Adele.

"And now, just one more thing! After seeing what the last war has done, let me ask you, Adele, what could be more beautiful than the whole world at peace with God, and with neighbor?"

"Nothing, sir, nothing! But when will that be?"

"When men will learn to come before the Face of the Lord and light a candle instead of a cannon!"

Suddenly Adele saw her master collapse in his chair. She summoned the doctor. It was a stroke of paralysis. Leo had to take to his bed.

Nearly all of the following year found Leo flat on his back or else propped with pillows in his large chair. Visitors seeking favors through the Holy Face, although much less numerous, still continued to trickle into the miracle room on the ground floor. Leo, however, remained in his suite upstairs, keeping himself informed on all that transpired before the Holy Face below.

However, he was not to remain strictly confined to his room. He had alternating periods of improvement, so that he was able to go downstairs to spend some time before his precious Image of the Saviour, and to speak a few words with visitors who still came for favors.

But Leo was no longer able to go to Mass, not even on Sundays. Once each week one of the priests from the Cathedral Church would bring him the Blessed Sacrament, and these were the days to which Leo would look forward. Then one day, the priest offered Leo a suggestion. "I would like to ask the Archbishop to give me permission to say Mass in your house, occasionally . . . ."

"No, Father, don't do that," Leo answered, pointedly.

"But I thought that would make you happy," the priest said, evidently puzzled.

"No, no, Father, do not speak of it."

"I only mentioned this because a friend of yours came to the rectory one day last week and told us how deeply you regretted being deprived of Mass. He told us you said no one could guess what it meant for you to surrender to this privation . . . ."

"Ah, yes, it is true. I said that in a moment of weakness. I felt I had to complain to someone. I never expected the news would reach you . . . ."

"But I am glad it did. Considering all the circumstances, I am certain the Archbishop will gladly give his permission to have Mass celebrated here occasionally."

"But, Father, I beg you, say nothing further about this. A wretched sinner, like me, ought not to reach out toward such an inestimable privilege. No! Is it not too much that our Lord should be troubled to come here once a week? Is it not enough that his priest must bother himself to make a trip all the way to St. Etienne Street to serve one unworthy sinner? I could never endure that the Church should be further troubled on my account . . . ."[70] Tears welled in the old man's eyes as he spoke.

During these months of his retirement, Leo continued to keep himself well posted on anything connected with the Church. Although his eyesight began to fail him, he became

70 *Ibid.*, p. 390.

at this late period of his life more interested in the press than he had ever been. He looked to Catholic editors and writers to defend the cause of the Church in modern times. With one hand paralyzed and another hardly able to move, he wrote repeated letters to them, recommending them for their efforts in denouncing liberal Catholicism.

But he was particularly without mercy toward authors of bad books. Denouncing them, he would write, "What a frightful abyss is opened under the feet of our youth by a wicked press!" He had a particular aptitude to notice taints of heretical leanings, freethinking, and liberalism in books that purported to be Catholic. "I am unfortunate," he wrote to a clerical friend, "when I take up a book, if there be any portion of it objectionable, I am certain at once to open it at that page."[71] Of Leo Dupont it could well be said that there was no sorrow, no joy, no fear or hope in any part of the Catholic world in which he did not interest himself.

To those who objected that living in grace was difficult, since the body clung after pleasure, Leo would say confidentially, "Why don't you take the advice of Father Lacordaire, our noted Dominican orator, and do as he recommends?" and then, straightaway initiating his hearers into Father Lacordaire's science, he would tell them, "The Father counsels us to fight back the temptations of the flesh with a good-sized whip. A few stinging lashes, self-inflicted, and lo, the craving for sensual pleasure goes! Father Lacordaire ought to know, for you see he continually lashes himself. Try it some time, and you will see that when you go away from the closet where you have lashed yourself even two or three times, you are a changed man . . . ."

If Leo recommended the discipline to others, it was because he had learned some forty years ago to use it on himself. As he used to walk down the street in his fine clothes, and with his polished manners, few would have suspected that this man who could afford rare luxuries chose to impose on his flesh the mortifying stings of a whip.

But the day came when Leo had to reconcile himself to

---

71 *Ibid.*, p. 406.

leave the miracle room, and to move upstairs permanently. A fresh attack of paralysis reduced him to the state of a helpless victim. Hardly able to hold a pen in his paralyzed hand, Leo still continued to write short letters and to copy prayers for the benefit of his friends, giving himself to the apostolate of the press which he so much valued—one last effort to do something for God. In one of these letters, Leo described what his sickroom had become to him. "Would you know what your room is? It is a little hermitage in the midst of a town, and you are the recluse; there you practise without witness or restraint your favorite devotions, you kiss the ground, you prostrate yourself, you strike your breast, you press your lips to the Sacred Wounds of the Amiable Saviour; in a word, you do all that a hermit can do in his desert. Would you know what your room is? It is a little temple, a chapel, of which you are the priest. The crucifix, the picture of the Mother of God and the holy water raise devout affections in your soul. Your heart is a burning lamp, consuming itself before the Lord. But, however great your solitude may be, remember that five persons are always present: God the Father, God the Son, God the Holy Ghost, your guardian angel and yourself. But remember also the saying of St. Gregory, the Great: 'What does exterior solitude avail if that of the heart be not well kept?' "

The suffering recluse on the second floor of St. Etienne Street seemed to have learned every lesson of the science of the saints. When, finally, both his hands became paralyzed and he could write no more, he looked at the volume of letters that still poured into his home, sorry that he could answer them no longer. Some wrote expressing their grief, and promising to pray for his recovery. Others, unaware of his grave illness, expressed their disappointment at his silence, and implored him to make some short reply. Leo, unable to oblige them, resigned himself to the inevitable; he would now be misunderstood, as his silence would be mistaken for indifference.

Only Adele, his faithful servant and companion, knew of Leo's physical suffering and his loneliness. She would sit at his side for hours and say the rosary with him, or read to him.

"Adele, you have buried all my dear ones. You will also have to receive my last sigh!"

"Oh, sir, my only regret will be to have to oblige you in this respect. I should have wished to precede you to heaven. But may God's will be done . . . ."

"The good Lord will give you strength to attend to everything when the time comes. Then, after I am gone, I want you to go to live with the Sisters. I have settled sufficiently on you to take care of you as long as you live . . . ."

"Oh, sir," sobbed Adele, wiping the tears from her wrinkled face. Then taking courage, she said, "Mr. Dupont, now that you are so low, I feel I should ask you something before it is too late . . . ."

"Speak, Adele. I'm listening."

"What about the Holy Face, sir?"

"What about it? Ah, Adele, I shall soon behold It glorious and resplendent in Heaven."

"But what about the Devotion? Who will carry it on after you are gone? Will it pass out of existence?"

"No, Adele. Sooner will heaven and earth pass away, than the Devotion to the Holy Face should pass out of existence."

"But, sir, there is no Papal Brief. And you know that Sister Marie Pierre said that without a Brief the Devotion would die!"

Leo seemed taken aback, as if stunned. He was at a loss for an answer.

"While you lived and kept up the Devotion here there was hope that some Bishop would come who would ask the Pope for a Brief. But three Bishops have been installed in Tours in the past thirty years, and still Sister Marie Pierre's life and revelations remain sealed up. Now it is three years since Archbishop Fruchaud has been here, yet no steps have been taken to unseal the buried treasure. You must admit it has been such a long time to wait."

"It looks hopeless, does it not, Adele?"

"Yes, it looks very hopeless."

"Then let us sink ourselves into the dust of our nothingness and ask God to show His power. We have worked the whole night and have taken nothing . . . ."

Then followed two weeks of such intense suffering for Leo that he was unable to be concerned about anything. He started to complain that his memory began to play him tricks, but those who attended him refused to agree with such a diagnosis. To them Leo appeared in full possession of his remarkable mental faculties. They felt it might have been another phase of the dark night of the soul, a helpless state of mental anxiety and interior trial, through which Leo would rise upward toward a new and higher degree of perfection.

Then one day Leo felt better. He seemed interested in what was going on.

"Adele, have I been dreaming, or did you tell me that we are to have a new Archbishop?"

"Yes, sir, I mentioned it to you a couple of days ago, but you seemed too ill to be concerned."

A fortnight later preparations for the installation of the new Ordinary of Tours, His Grace Archbishop Colet, were in progress.

"Look, Adele, the poor pilgrim is being invited to the Archbishop's installation ceremonies, and to a banquet later. . . . I am good for nothing but to lay here motionless."

"But it is nice to get an invitation written in His Grace's own handwriting," beamed Adele.

"You say His Grace wrote it out himself?" asked Leo.

"That is what the Vicar told me when he read it to you."

"His Grace is a humble man to be bothered about a useless old creature like myself."

The winter passed by without any noticeable change in Leo's physical condition. He was weak, paralyzed, bed-ridden; but he was not dying. He kept holding on to life by some inexplicable grasp, and nobody understood what it was that kept him alive.

Then one day in early spring, Leo had a caller. "Say nothing to Mr. Dupont. Just take me to his room for a brief visit . . . ." It was His Grace Archbishop Colet, himself, and

Adele, though visibly flustered, led the prelate obediently to the room on the second floor.

"His Excellency, Archbishop Colet, is here to visit you, sir," said Adele nervously.

"I have come to call on you, and to give you my blessing. I am so sorry that you are ill."

Leo appeared embarrassed. To be visited by the new Archbishop in his condition was something he did not expect. The prelate made himself so pleasant and gracious that Leo lost his self-consciousness. Warm and understanding, Archbishop Colet hovered over the paralyzed invalid, whispering words of comfort and encouragement. Finally, when he was ready to leave, he said amusingly, "You see, Mr. Dupont, it is no use evading the bishop. If you will not come to his house, he will come to yours . . . ."

"Thank you, Your Grace, thank you so much."

The Archbishop then placed both his hands on the aged man's head and pronounced the words of benediction. Leo only looked up gratefully at the prelate, unable to say a word. Adele then politely escorted His Excellency to the door. When she returned to Leo's room, she found him jubilant.

"Adele, I think I see a spark of hope," he said, confidentially.

"You mean, for the Devotion to the Holy Face?"

"Yes," replied Leo.

"Well, sir, I've been disappointed too long and too often to be optimistic now. I have lived too long to allow myself to be encouraged too easily."

"I'm ashamed of you, Adele. If you can't tell at one glance that Archbishop Colet is a saint and a most extraordinary man, I am afraid I have to disagree with you!"

"Not that, sir. Let it never be said that there was any disagreement between us. If you have hope, sir, I too have hope."

"Very well, then, Adele, and to prove your sincerity I want you to go downstairs and kneel before the picture of the Holy Face and thank our Saviour for Bishop Colet!"

Adele did as she was told, and as she prayed she thought the light in the lamp flickered a bit more brightly. She re-

called vividly what Leo Dupont had told her three years ago
when she wondered if ever some bishop would approve the
Work of Reparation. "Whoever the Bishop will be, he will
surely come some day, Adele, and he will light the candle
which we kept flickering before the Holy Face these past
years . . . ."

Six months later, the Chaplain of the Carmelite Sisters
came to the house on the Rue St. Etienne, his face beaming
with joy, as he demanded that Adele take him upstairs.

"But, please, please," urged Adele, "try to be more composed. Mr. Dupont is very feeble and ill. Whatever the news
you have, please break it slowly."

"But it is wonderful news. It is the news Mr. Dupont has
waited to hear for thirty years!"

"The more reason for caution. Mr. Dupont is not at all
strong," she counseled as she led the priest to the sickroom
on the second floor.

"The chaplain from the Carmelite Monastery has come to
pay you a little visit, sir," announced Adele, beckoning the
priest to appear casual.

"Ah, the Carmelite Monastery! It is always in my thoughts.
How often I look out of my window through which I can
see part of it. 'Behold, how Carmel shines!' I exclaim to myself many times during the course of a day. And tell me,
Father, how are the Sisters?"

"They are well and send their regards and assurances of
prayers," answered the chaplain, constraining himself by
great effort to appear calm.

"Carmel," went on Leo, "is the Church's highest estate.
Do you realize that it was on the Feast of Our Lady of Mount
Carmel that Our Lady appeared to Bernadette for the last
time? Yes, from Carmel where souls are in endless contact
with the Divine will come graces to the world quite unexpectedly and in greatest surprise . . . ."

"Speaking of surprises from Carmel, Mr. Dupont, I believe
I have a surprise you will be happy to hear about . . . ."

"Tell me about it, Father. I am so glad you came. I haven't
felt as strong as I feel today for a long while. Now what is this
surprise you bring?"

"It is about Sister Marie Pierre . . . ."

"Sister Marie Pierre?" Leo had not expected this.

"Yes, her life and revelations have been approved!"

"But when and how was it done?" asked Leo excitedly.

"By Archbishop Colet," replied the priest. "His Grace has given orders to unseal the archives and to bring out all the documents concerning the life and revelations of Sister Marie Pierre, so that he could personally examine them. Having read every work, the Archbishop was so edified with everything that he sent the documents by special messenger to the learned Benedictine Fathers at the Abbey of Solesmes for their study and analysis . . . ."

"*Sit Nomen Domini benedictum!*" was all that Leo could say.

"But that is not all! The documents have just been returned by the Benedictines with the highest recommendations. And Archbishop Colet, anxious to see the Work of Reparation to the Holy Face begun, urges that the life and revelations of Sister Marie Pierre be published!"

Leo was silent for awhile, and then in a clear, audible voice he said, "Now dost Thou dismiss Thy servant in peace, oh, Lord, for my eyes have seen the salvation of the world!"

Leo Dupont was ready to die. The favor for which he had hoped and prayed for thirty years was being granted. The Work of Reparation which the Saviour had in mind when He said, *The most beautiful work under the sun is about to dawn,* was actually beginning to see the light of day. And now that the dawn was breaking, Leo was ready to look toward the setting sun

A few days later, Leo asked for his cousin from Chissay. When he arrived, he found Leo very weak but in full consciousness.

"I am near the end of my pilgrimage, Cousin Marolles, and I want you to attend to my will," Leo told him calmly.

He grew steadily weaker, and soon it was difficult to understand his speech.

"Cousin, I desire to have the . . . good . . . ."

"What, what is it you wish?" Mr. Marolles asked him, trying to make him out, but without success. Adele was called in.

"Sir, what is it that you wish?" she asked him, bending over his bed.

"I desire to have the . . . good . . . God . . . ." came in muffled tones which Adele, accustomed to his speech, readily understood.

"Very well, sir, the priest shall be sent for and I will make ready a little wedding-feast, as we did for Madame," she answered. She meant the arrangement of a small sick-call altar adorned with wax candles and fresh flowers.

Just before high noon, the priest arrived and Leo, although unable to swallow any food, received the host with great ease and much devotion. Later he was given Extreme Unction, following every part of the sacred rite with attention and his habitual piety.

Two days later, Leo, usually so tranquil, appeared in great distress. He called for Adele. "It is the wicked serpent, Adele! The wretch has been trying to make me promises. He torments me . . . ."

"Have no fear, sir," replied the old servant, who remembered all the lessons she had learned from her loving master. "Say to the devil, *'Vade, retro, Satana.'* You remember how the Master urged Sister Marie Pierre to use these words with which to send Satan back to the pit where he belongs . . . ."

Leo repeated the words with emphasis.

"Now I will sprinkle you with holy water," said Adele, after which she offered him a holy water font, saying, "Take some on your finger and cross yourself, sir," which he obediently did.

All during the following day, the adversary of mankind kept renewing his assaults against the dying man.

"Adele, some more holy water," Leo would say in his defective speech and Adele at once would make the aspersions. At the end of the day, however, the wicked one departed, and the holy man was to be troubled no more. The hour in which Satan had been allowed to do his wicked works was past.

[199]

Calmly, serenely, Leo continued to murmur his prayers.

On Friday evening, March 17, Adele thought the end was near. She summoned the other two servants who were in the house, Zepheryn, who had been with Leo Dupont for fourteen years, and Adelaide, the cook, who had served him twenty-eight years. They knelt at his bedside, Leo's small adopted family, whom he treated more as his children than his servants. They begged him to pray for them, and they assured him they would continue to have Devotion to the Holy Face, as he had taught it to them.

Early the following morning, as the sky became slightly lighted by the approach of the rising sun, Leo Dupont breathed his last breath. It was Saturday, March 18, 1876. He was seventy-nine years old.

Mr. Marolles, who was executor of Leo's last will, took charge of interment.

The body of the adorer of the Holy Face was laid out in the parlor where hung the picture of the Vera Effigies, before which so many miracles had taken place. A steady stream of people came to the house on St. Etienne Street to view for the last time the remains of Leo Dupont, throughout the day on Saturday and all through Sunday until Monday morning at ten o'clock, the hour appointed for the funeral. Many touched their rosaries, medals, and prayerbooks to his hands, believing that he, who during life was the instrument through whom God had granted extraordinary favors to countless persons, would also after death prove a powerful intercessor.

Although Leo Dupont had requested a quiet funeral, enjoining his cousin not to invite persons to follow him to the grave, the occasion of his obsequies was quite the reverse. His funeral was a sort of religious triumph, one of those public demonstrations spontaneously brought about by sanctity. Not only did all the ecclesiastical dignitaries of Tours attend the funeral, but religious communities, as well as the principal citizens of the town, were present.

When the funeral cortege arrived at the cemetery where Leo's remains, according to his express wish, were to be buried in a grave alongside the graves of his daughter and his mother, some thought it fitting to make a few remarks:

"A saint like Leo Dupont ought to be buried in a special place . . . ."

"Yes, under the church, or the cathedral . . . ."

"Well, mark my word, a day will come when his body will be removed and will receive all the honors he deserves . . . ."

THE DEATH OF LEO DUPONT

27

WHEN, one month after the death of Leo Dupont, the house at 8 Rue St. Etienne was put up for sale, public reaction to this news flared high in all sections of Tours. Most of the city's Catholic population were concerned that the house in which so many miracles had been worked might pass into careless or even profane hands. They lost no time in voicing their protests to the executor of Leo Dupont's will, Mr. Marolles, who, defending his stand, declared he had no alternative since it devolved upon him to close out the estate.

When news of the proposed sale reached the Carmelite Monastery, the Sisters decided to intervene. Although quite poor, they had recently been favored with a substantial contribution, and they now appealed to the Archbishop to use the sum to buy the famous house on the Rue St. Etienne. This proposal met with the Prelate's complete and prompt approval.

Finally, when it seemed to Mr. Marolles that as executor he had attended faithfully to the explicit provisions of his cousin's last will and testament, he found himself confronted with one remaining problem. Whereas Leo Dupont's will clearly stipulated the disposition of even some of the minor objects of piety which belonged to Leo, it said nothing about what was to be done with the picture of the Holy Face which hung in his house and which had gained world-wide fame. One short sentence in the will indicated, however, that the servant of the Holy Face was much concerned about the venerated picture: "It is from no forgetfulness on my part, if I do not speak in my will of the Holy Face Picture. I do not wish to take part in the questions which may arise when

I am no longer there to trim the lamps of my oratory. God will provide for this according to His Holy Will . . . ."

And God *did* provide in a way that would have surpassed the highest hopes and anticipations of the testator. For Archbishop Colet, who so wholeheartedly endorsed the Carmelites for offering to purchase the house on Rue St. Etienne, now offered to take formal steps to convert the private domicile of the Holy Man of Tours into a public oratory.

Issuing a formal Ordinance, the Archbishop proclaimed that he would himself in person solemnly bless and inaugurate the new Oratory in which the servant of God, Leo Dupont, had for so many years kept a lamp burning day and night before a portrait of the Holy Face of Our Redeemer, and where so many marvelous prodigies have been wrought through anointing with the oil of the lamp.

Workmen were at once hired to do such remodeling as seemed necessary to convert the private dwelling into a public oratory. The parlor where the Picture of the Holy Face hung, and the room adjoining it, which was the dining hall, were made into one large room by the removal of the partition wall. This room was to be the Oratory. Here an altar was erected.

"It is from no forgetfulness on my part, if I do not speak in my will of the Holy Face Picture . . . . God will provide for this according to His Holy Will," wrote Leo in his Last Will and Testament, and now only three months after his death, the Picture of the Holy Face, encased in a new frame of gilt bronze and studded with precious stones, was hanging over the altar in the new Oratory. The day was June 29, 1876. Gathered on the Rue St. Etienne was a large concourse of clergy, superiors of religious communities, and Catholic laity. At the altar was Archbishop Colet, himself the first to offer the Sacrifice of Mass in the Oratory which had been the home of the Holy Man of Tours. In the course of the sermon which His Grace delivered that morning, there echoed two names, that of Sister Marie Pierre, the mystic of Carmel, and that of Leo Dupont, her ardent collaborator, who set his goal to propagate her mission. "It was Sister Marie Pierre who had inspired the Work of Reparation, which in a touching form had been practiced for so many years in this ever blessed place, the house of the servant of God, Leo Dupont . . . ."

The Prelate's inspired sermon warmed the hearts of his hearers as it urged them to imitate the example of the two Adorers of the Holy Face. Adele Colombe, the mulatto servant of the Holy Man of Tours, kneeling in a back pew, marveled at the wonderful ways of God. It was only one year ago that she complained to Leo Dupont, telling him the whole thing seemed so hopeless. Three Bishops had succeeded to the See of St. Martin and all passed by unnoticed the Work of Reparation to the Holy Face, while the solitary pilgrim on Rue St. Etienne was left to carry on by himself as best he could for thirty long years. Then, during the few weeks of life that remained to Leo, a fourth Archbishop coming upon the scene approved the revelations of Sister Marie Pierre and thus crowned the career of Leo Dupont.

As if that were not in itself a culminating triumph, now, only three months after his death, his parlor had become a sanctuary in which the Archbishop himself was offering the Sacrifice of the Mass. Hopeless? It turned out to be hopeful in a degree no one could have imagined. "I have trusted in the Lord; I shall not be confounded forever," Adele repeated to herself again and again.

At this dramatic point of climax in the launching of the Work of Reparation, another ecclesiastic, equally as zealous as Archbishop Colet, but without his deep supernatural prudence, might at once have petitioned the Holy See for a New Brief, that would approve Devotion to the Holy Face in connection with Reparation. But Archbishop Colet had drawn up another plan. Ultimately, he would have recourse to the Supreme Pontiff, and beg of the Vicar of Christ to endorse the Cult of the Holy Face. But for the present, Archbishop Colet decided to first make the life and the mission of Sister Marie Pierre and her saintly disciple, Leo Dupont, known to the world by means of the press. The Saviour Himself had asked Sister Marie Pierre to promote the work by means of the printed word. The Cult would spread, promised Our Lord, if the Work were properly explained in leaflets and booklets.

Accordingly, Archbishop Colet now appointed a chaplain to attend to the Oratory on St. Etienne Street, now called The Oratory of the Holy Face. From this Oratory, pamphlets and booklets bearing his "imprimatur" were to be disseminated throughout the diocese, and in due time further into France, so that the Catholic faithful could learn of the exalted revelations of Sister Marie Pierre, and become acquainted with the miracles received through Devotion to the Holy Face in Leo Dupont's home.

The response to this avalanche of leaflets and booklets was spontaneous and overwhelming. The demand for more literature dealing with the Work of Reparation increased, and pilgrimages to the Oratory of the Holy Face multiplied. Aware that it was not enough to have only one priest attending to the Work, Archbishop Colet formed a diocesan Society of Priests who were to reside in the holy house on Rue St. Etienne under a rule, with the purpose of dedicating their lives to the spread of the Cult of the Holy Face. They were to be known as Priests of the Holy Face.

But if this new community were to grow and prosper in their mission, it was necessary to select a capable superior to direct them. Archbishop Charles Colet, who never lost sight of the fact that the press was to be the principal means of promoting Reparation to the Holy Face, since the Saviour Himself had asked that the Work be explained and furthered through the printed word, knew that the head of the new community would have to be a practical-minded man who could interest himself in the numerous details involved in the successful management of modern printing, and who also had literary abilities.

Father Peter Janvier answered this description, and Archbishop Colet installed him as the first director of the new community, with the understanding that the new Director would begin at once to collate facts and data on the lives of the two adorers of the Holy Face with a view to publishing at the earliest possible date two full-length biographies, one the Life of Sister Marie Pierre, and the other the Life of the venerable Leo Dupont.

The timing of this project was perfect, for it was only two

years since the death of Leo Dupont, and his memory was alive everywhere. Moreover, Father Janvier had known Leo personally for many years, and he was not disposed to any expedient measure of haphazard guessing as to Leo's real virtues and deeds. Unlike the writing of the lives of saints who lived two or three hundred years ago, making the biographical task an arduous one, it was not difficult to obtain real facts on the lives of Sister Marie Pierre and Leo Dupont, for they were contemporaries of whom every one spoke familiarly and knowingly.

Working day and night, Father Janvier spared no pains or research to make his biographies complete and correct. In the meantime, the Catholic Faithful, having read the many small pamphlets and booklets treating the Work of Reparation, were eager for a full story of the lives of the two servants of the Holy Face. As early as 1879, an edition of the *Life of Leo Dupont* came from the press, and by 1881, less than five years after the death of Leo, dual publications treating the full life stories of the two adorers of the Holy Face, bearing the "imprimatur" of Archbishop Colet and also a preface attesting his fullest endorsement and encouragement, were given out to the public.

No sooner had the French-speaking Catholics read the biographies by Father Janvier, than requests poured in from foreign countries, asking for translations. Without delay, Father Janvier's two monumental books were rendered into English, Spanish, and German. As early as 1882, only six years after Leo's death, the English-speaking peoples of Great Britain and the United States were given English versions of the lives of Sister Marie Pierre and her zealous spiritual accomplice, Leo Dupont.

To these English translations a group of American Bishops hastened to give their fullest approval. Among these members of the Hierarchy was Cardinal Gibbons of Baltimore, who gave the folowing approbation in writing: "The Life of the devout Carmelite of Tours is calculated to promote piety and edification not only in cloistered Institutions, but also in the ranks of secular life."

Similarly wrote the Most Reverend William H. Gross,

Bishop of Savannah, the Most Reverend William Henry Elder, Archbishop of Cincinnati, and others, as they each gave their fullest ecclesiastical approval to spread far and wide the Worship of the Holy Face.

But, perhaps, the chief among the propagators of the Work of Reparation to the Holy Face in the United States was the Archbishop of New Orleans, Louisiana, the Most Reverend Napoleon Perche, who, not content to give a written approbation to Sister Marie Pierre's mission, made a personal visit to the Oratory of the Holy Face in Tours, and there became personally acquainted with the facts of the wonders that took place in the ancient city of St. Martin. Perhaps because the Archbishop from New Orleans was himself a Frenchman, he was more inclined to be interested in the graces of which his native France had been the favored recipient. So deeply was Archbishop Perche impressed by all he learned at Tours, that on returning to his see he at once proceeded canonically to establish a Confraternity of Reparation to the Holy Face in his own diocese, appropriately selecting the Chapel of the Discalced Carmelite Nuns for this singular privilege. This was destined to be the first chapel in the new world where Devotion to the Holy Face was to find its beginning. Over the high altar a true copy of the "Vera Effigies" was erected.[72] To the Carmelite Monastery of New Orleans was thus entrusted the extension of the Work of Reparation in the New World.

The candle that had been lighted before the Holy Face had by now reached its brilliance across the broad Atlantic, and Archbishop Colet, noting the admirable response of the Catholic Faithful to the Work of the Reparation, now felt the hour had come for him to appeal to the Pope for the Brief which would validly perpetuate the Work of the Holy Face until the end of time.

But as he set himself to this task which was to crown his Episcopate of Reparation, Archbishop Colet became ill. After a brief sickness, he passed away quietly to contemplate in

---

72 *Manual of the Devotion of Reparation to the Holy Face by the Discalced Carmelite Nuns, New Orleans, Louisiana,* p. 16.

Heaven that Holy Face which he had worshiped here below, overcoming all obstacles to make it loved and adored throughout the world.

A few months later, Archbishop William Meignan was installed as the new Bishop of Tours, and many who remembered the thirty years of silence imposed on the Revelations of Sister Marie Pierre, prayed for the triumph of their cause under the new bishop. How would he view the Work of Reparation? Whatever the new developments, there was no turning back the tide, for the Work, having been bolstered with an adequate press and a canonically established Oratory, was no longer to meet with the frowning disapproval of the past.

Archbishop William Meignan did not long leave the faithful of his diocese in doubt as to his intentions. Within the short space of a few months, the new Archbishop issued a lengthy Ordinance establishing The Confraternity of the Holy Face in the Oratory on the Rue St. Etienne. A few months later, the Archbishop secured from the Supreme Pontiff an apostolic letter granting special indulgences to the members of the Confraternity. The time was now ripe to petition the Holy See for a Brief that would raise the Confraternity of the Holy Face to the rank of Archconfraternity and thus insure its perpetuity.

Archbishop Meignan drew up a plan of action. His Grace appointed Father Janvier, the Director of the Oratory, to write a petition begging the Holy Father for this favor, and then urged that the petition be first sent to the Hierarchy in all parts of the world, asking them to affix their signatures recommending the petition to His Holiness.

Nearly sixty bishops and archbishops from France, Belgium, Italy, Spain, Switzerland, Austria, England, Ireland, the United States, and Canada hastened to sign their names recommending the petition to Pope Leo XIII.

Devotion to the Holy Face was destined to become an integral part of Divine worship in the Church. It now seemed certain that the sea of arguments so long raised against Sister Marie Pierre's revelations were to disappear into thin air.

When the Pope read the petition, he looked with surprise

at the long list of familiar episcopal names urging approval of Devotion to the Holy Face by raising the association to the dignity of an Archconfraternity. Attentively, the Holy Father studied the names, but when, at the end of the long list, he saw the names of seven members of the American hierarchy in support of the cause, His Holiness was gratified beyond words at the extension of devotion to the Saviour. Slowly Leo XIII read the names of the American Bishops— there were the signatures of His Eminence Cardinal McCloskey, Archbishop of New York; Archbishop Gibbons of Baltimore, Archbishop Elder of Cincinnati, Bishop Keane of Richmond, Bishop Neraz of San Antonio, and Bishop Jansens of Natchez (later to become Archbishop of New Orleans).

According to the customs of the Court of Rome, the favor solicited in the petition could not be granted at once, but would have to come in degrees and in successive portions. For example, the power of attaching or aggregating would have to be granted first to the Diocese of Tours, later France, then some neighboring countries, until at last it would come to include the whole world.

Accordingly, the Prefect of the Sacred Congregation of Rites present at the audience of the Holy Father asked if the title of Archconfraternity could be granted then and there for all of France, *"pro Gallia."*

Pope Leo XIII looked up, and then, without a moment's pause, sat down and wrote, *"Non tam pro Gallia, quam ubique."* Not only for all of France, but for the whole world! Rome had spoken. An irrevocable verdict had been pronounced.

When news of this unprecedented favor reached Tours by telegram, it seemed so incredible that the Fathers at the Oratory thought it best to maintain silence, until written confirmation of the developments would become available.

A few days later, an official document entitled, "Brief of His Holiness Pope Leo XIII, establishing The Archconfraternity of the Holy Face," was forwarded to Tours. The mission of Sister Marie Pierre had been realized. *Without the formality of a Brief the Work would die,* said the Saviour to

Sister Marie Pierre, urging her to work for a solid foundation. Now that the Work had a Brief, it could never die!

The Priests of the Holy Face at the Oratory had good cause to rejoice as they read alternate parts of the Brief which gave them the privilege in perpetuity to lawfully receive members into their Archconfraternity from all over the world.

"We decree that our present letters shall be for the present and for the future, fixed, valid and efficacious," read the Brief. "Any power and authority to judge and interpret otherwise is taken away from all ordinary judges and delegates whoever they may be, whether they be Nuncios of the Holy See, Cardinals of the Holy Roman Church, or even legates a latere, and all other persons whatever their dignity and their power may be; so that if any one, whatever the authority with which he is invested, attacks any of these clauses knowingly or through ignorance, his act shall be null and void.

"Given at Rome, near St. Peter, under the ring of the fisherman, the 1st day of October, 1885, being the 8th year of our pontificate. Signed, Cardinal Ledochowski."

✦   ✦

So dawned upon the earth the Devotion to the Holy Face, of which the Saviour said that *it was the most beautiful work under the sun.* Thousands of Catholics in all walks of life sent in petitions to be inscribed in the New Archconfraternity of the Holy Face, as parish after parish in various dioceses of the Catholic world begged to have a confraternity affiliated with that of Tours.

The Brief of Leo XIII had settled for all the Faithful, and for all time to come, the validity and efficacy of the Devotion to the Holy Face in Catholic worship. No voice could be raised against it anymore, anywhere in the world. As in the century preceding when Devotion to the Sacred Heart took its rightful place in Catholic worship as a means of arousing Catholics from their coldness and indifference, so now Devotion to the Holy Face was to make reparation for the sins and crimes of modern disbelievers and of militant atheism on the march.

Think of the outrages inflicted on Me by the Society of Communists, the enemies of the Church and of her Christ! complained Our Divine Saviour to Sister Marie Pierre. *They have laid their hands upon the anointed of the Lord. But their machinations are vain; their designs shall be foiled.*[73] *I DESIRE THE ESTABLISHMENT OF THE WORK OF REPARATION! For it is the Work of Reparation to the Holy Face that will disarm God's justice.*

---

73 *Life of Sister Marie Pierre*, p. 296.

ORATORY IN THE HOME OF LEO DUPONT

At the left is the celebrated picture of the Holy Face, before
which Leo Dupont kept a lamp burning day and night. At the
right is the Holy Bible he used during his lifetime, and which
he also honored with a lamp. The crutches at the right were
left by victims after praying before the Holy Face.

BIBLIOGRAPHY

The Devotion to the Holy Face at Saint Peter's of the Vatican, PETER JANVIER, translated from the French by A. B. Bennett, 1894.

The Life of Leon Papin-Dupont, the Holy Man of Tours, edited by EDWARD HEALY THOMPSON, Burns and Oates, 1882.

Life of Sister Marie de St. Pierre of the Holy Family, SISTER M. EMMANUEL, O.S.B., Burns, Oates and Washbourne, 1938.

Life of Sister Marie Pierre, PETER JANVIER, translated from the French by Henri Le Mercier de Pombiray, 1884

Manual of the Confraternity of the Holy Face, by the Discalced Carmelite Nuns, New Orleans 16, Louisiana, 1947.

M. Dupont, PETER JANVIER, translated from the French by Christian Reid, 1886.

Oratoire de la Sainte Face, Tours, 1877.

If you have enjoyed this book, consider making your next selection from among the following . . .

St. Vincent Ferrer. *Fr. Pradel, O.P.* 9.00
The Life of Father De Smet. *Fr. Laveille, S.J.* 18.00
Glories of Divine Grace. *Fr. Matthias Scheeben* 18.00
Holy Eucharist—Our All. *Fr. Lukas Etlin.* 3.00
Hail Holy Queen (from *Glories of Mary*). *St. Alphonsus* 9.00
Novena of Holy Communions. *Lovasik* 2.50
Brief Catechism for Adults. *Cogan.* 12.50
The Cath. Religion—Illus./Expl. for Child, Adult, Convert. *Burbach* 12.50
Eucharistic Miracles. *Joan Carroll Cruz.* 16.50
The Incorruptibles. *Joan Carroll Cruz* 16.50
Secular Saints: 250 Lay Men, Women & Children. PB. *Cruz.* 35.00
Pope St. Pius X. *F. A. Forbes* 11.00
St. Alphonsus Liguori. *Frs. Miller and Aubin* 18.00
Self-Abandonment to Divine Providence. *Fr. de Caussade, S.J.* 22.50
The Song of Songs—A Mystical Exposition. *Fr. Arintero, O.P.* 21.50
Prophecy for Today. *Edward Connor* 7.50
Saint Michael and the Angels. *Approved Sources* 9.00
Dolorous Passion of Our Lord. *Anne C. Emmerich.* 18.00
Modern Saints—Their Lives & Faces, Book I. *Ann Ball.* 21.00
Modern Saints—Their Lives & Faces, Book II. *Ann Ball* 23.00
Our Lady of Fatima's Peace Plan from Heaven. *Booklet.* 1.00
Divine Favors Granted to St. Joseph. *Père Binet.* 7.50
St. Joseph Cafasso—Priest of the Gallows. *St. John Bosco.* 6.00
Catechism of the Council of Trent. *McHugh/Callan.* 27.50
The Foot of the Cross. *Fr. Faber.* 18.00
The Rosary in Action. *John Johnson* 12.00
Padre Pio—The Stigmatist. *Fr. Charles Carty* 16.50
Why Squander Illness? *Frs. Rumble & Carty* 4.00
The Sacred Heart and the Priesthood. *de la Touche* 10.00
Fatima—The Great Sign. *Francis Johnston* 12.00
Heliotropium—Conformity of Human Will to Divine. *Drexelius* 15.00
Charity for the Suffering Souls. *Fr. John Nageleisen* 18.00
Devotion to the Sacred Heart of Jesus. *Verheylezoon* 16.50
Who Is Padre Pio? *Radio Replies Press* 3.00
The Stigmata and Modern Science. *Fr. Charles Carty* 2.50
St. Anthony—The Wonder Worker of Padua. *Stoddard.* 7.00
The Precious Blood. *Fr. Faber.* 16.50
The Holy Shroud & Four Visions. *Fr. O'Connell* 3.50
Clean Love in Courtship. *Fr. Lawrence Lovasik* 4.50
The Secret of the Rosary. *St. Louis De Montfort.* 5.00
The History of Antichrist. *Rev. P. Huchede.* 4.00
St. Catherine of Siena. *Alice Curtayne* 16.50
Where We Got the Bible. *Fr. Henry Graham* 8.00
Hidden Treasure—Holy Mass. *St. Leonard.* 7.50
Imitation of the Sacred Heart of Jesus. *Fr. Arnoudt* 18.50
The Life & Glories of St. Joseph. *Edward Thompson.* 16.50
Père Lamy. *Biver.* 15.00
Humility of Heart. *Fr. Cajetan da Bergamo* 9.00
The Curé D'Ars. *Abbé Francis Trochu* 24.00
Love, Peace and Joy. (St. Gertrude). *Prévot* 8.00

At your Bookdealer or direct from the Publisher.
Toll-Free 1-800-437-5876   *Fax 815-226-7770*

Prices subject to change.

THE "GOLDEN ARROW" PRAYER

MAY the most holy, most sacred, most adorable, most incomprehensible and unutterable Name of God be always praised, blessed, loved, adored and glorified, in Heaven, on earth, and under the earth, by all the creatures of God, and by the Sacred Heart of Our Lord Jesus Christ in the Most Holy Sacrament of the Altar. Amen.

After receiving this prayer, Sister Mary of St. Peter was given a vision in which she saw the Sacred Heart of Jesus delightfully wounded by this *"Golden Arrow,"* as torrents of graces streamed from It for the conversion of sinners.